2022

上海虹桥国际中央商务区

发展报告

2022 Annual Report on Development of Shanghai Hongqiao International CBD

上海虹桥国际中央商务区管理委员会　编

上海社会科学院出版社
SHANGHAI ACADEMY OF SOCIAL SCIENCES PRESS

编审委员会

编写工作组

序

  2022年是贯彻落实《虹桥国际开放枢纽建设总体方案》(简称《总体方案》)重要之年。这一年,《上海市促进虹桥国际中央商务区发展条例》《上海虹桥国际中央商务区产业发展规划》《上海虹桥国际中央商务区国土空间中近期规划》先后发布,从制度体系、产业体系、规划体系进行顶层设计,为商务区未来发展夯基垒台、架梁立柱。

  面对百年变局和世纪疫情,虹桥国际中央商务区全面深入贯彻中央决策部署,紧扣一体化、高质量和国际化,突出总部经济能级提升、突出贸易功能内涵拓展、突出流量价值挖掘和创造,高效统筹区域疫情防控和经济社会发展,全面推进虹桥国际开放枢纽建设总体方案落地落实,"七个专项行动"和经济发展三年倍增目标稳步推进,商务区作为"极中极""彩虹桥"的功能和作用进一步显现。

  这一年,商务区在上海市委、市政府的坚强领导下,准确把握自身定位和比较优势,精准发力打开招商引资新局面,启动实施虹桥国际商务伙伴计划,会同四区到皖浙等地举办长三角企业家圆桌会,全面打响投资虹桥品牌。制定实施贸易型总部、民营总部等一批创新性政策措施,强化资源禀赋打造总部经济新格局,形成特色鲜明的"四高五新"产业发展规划,推动区域经济跑出加速度。加快配套性建设力度,提升区域城市品质,完善区域交通体系,持续推动虹桥国际商务人才港、人力资源产业园和国际中央法务区建设,推动上海市"一带一路"综合服务中心、知识产权保护中心虹桥工作站和RCEP企业服务咨询站等专业化服务功能落地，打造服务"一带一路"桥头堡，为各类企业"走出去"提供专业服务支撑。

面向全球、展望未来，着眼"四个放在"，从全球、全国、长三角、全市四个维度看，商务区未来战略定位是联通世界的亚太流量枢纽港、全国统一大市场的关键节点、长三角一体化发展的新引擎、上海强劲活跃增长的动力源，成为名副其实的长三角经济地理中心。要进一步深化对战略内涵的认识，切实承担长三角一体化发展战略重要承载区、中国国际进口博览会永久举办地的使命任务，发挥长三角企业进入上海的门户功能和走向世界的桥头堡功能，努力在贯彻落实国家战略中当好排头兵、先行者，把虹桥国际开放枢纽建设宏伟蓝图转化为施工图、实景画。

本书的编撰，得到了上海社会科学院专业团队的支持。希望通过《2022上海虹桥国际中央商务区发展报告》这本书，让更多的人了解虹桥、关注虹桥、热爱虹桥，与虹桥国际中央商务区共创美好未来。

虹桥国际中央商务区管理委员会　党组书记　常务副主任

目　　录

第一章　经济"稳增长"

第一节　背景形势

一、国际层面

2022年，全球经济形势和地缘政治格局发生了深刻的变化，无论是从区域分布、周期演变趋势还是从供需结构上看，全球经济下行压力均在增大，经济增速逐季放缓。新冠疫情影响深远，世界主要经济体经济下行风险加大，全球滞胀风险上升，主要经济体政策收缩力度加快。与此同时，危机与机遇并存，全球科技和产业革命加速酝酿，技术进步和产业升级持续演进，绿色转型和可持续发展方兴未艾，全球经济正处于新旧动能转换和结构调整关键期。

新冠疫情对全球价值链和国际贸易的冲击，仍将是全球贸易今后面临的突出问题。以复杂价值链联系为特征的行业，尤其是电子和汽车产品行业，其贸易下降幅度可能会更大。疫情使全球产业链、供应链面临断链危机，跨国公司更加注重寻求就近化和属地化的供应链重构，推动产业链布局"更加永久性的改变"。疫情促进了互联网、大数据与传统外贸产业相结合，加快了服务贸易数字化进程，促使贸易形态更加多样化。

全球经贸体系正加速重构。当前逆全球化思潮抬头，单边主义、保护主义明显上升，世界进入新的动荡变革期。美国主导的"印太经济框架"（IPEF）、欧盟"全球门户"（Global Gateway）计划陆续出台，《全面与进步跨太平洋伙伴关系协定》（CPTPP）、《数字经济伙伴关系协定》（DEPA）等高标准经贸协定成为国家/地区发展新诉求。从长远看，中美贸易关系将长期处于竞争合作的博弈过程中，进入"有管理的全面竞争"；中俄、中欧关系愈加重要且复杂，未来中欧在数字转型和绿色发展等领域合作前景宽广。

新一轮产业变革重塑产业竞争版图。当前在全球蓬勃兴起的新一轮产业变革由以信息技术为核心的一组通用技术的成熟、扩散和深度融合为引领，对工业化大生产时代所构筑的生产方式、市场模式和企业组织关系等产生了深刻影响。发达国家依靠基础性技术掌控新兴产业竞争主导权的意图强烈，在信息、能源、环境、生物、制造、海洋、空间等产业领域，美国掌控大多数的基础性技术。新一轮产业变革新形势下，需求端的市场规模、需求主体的多元化构成、需求内容的差异化水平等，在很大程度上决定新兴产业的发展空间。新一轮产业变革所具有的数字化、智能化技术特征，使得以先进技术装备替代劳动力的成本经济性逐步显现，可能重塑世界产业竞争版图。

二、国家层面

对外开放是推动我国经济社会发展的重要动力，以开放促改革、促发展是我国发展不断取得新成就的重要法宝。习近平总书记高度重视对外开放工作，明确指出开放是当代中国的鲜明标识，强调"中国开放的大门不会关闭，只会越开越大"。在2022年第五届进博会开幕式视频讲话中也指出，开放是人类文明进步的重要动力，是世界繁荣发展的必由之路。党的二十大报告中指出，要"推进高水平对外开放。依托我国超大规模市场优势，以国内大循环吸引全球资源要素，增强国内国际两个市场两种资源联动效应，提升贸易投资合作质量和水平。稳步扩大规则、规制、管理、标准等制度型开放"。

2022年，我国新冠疫情反复，从供给和需求两端冲击经济，预期减弱，经济环境剧变，下行压力骤增。疫情防控难度比2020年更大，统筹疫情防控和经济社会发展难度增加，企业生产经营的困难比较突出。面对这些困难和挑战，国内防疫政策不断优化，助企纾困，扩大国内需求，稳增长政策力度持续加大，温和可控的物价水平为宏观政策灵活操作提供充足空间，出口仍有较强支撑，随着这些政策措施的逐步显效，经济将延续恢复发展态势。

外贸发展成绩斐然，引进外资和对外投资成果显著。面对复杂变化的国内外形势和新冠疫情冲击，我国对外贸易仍然展现出强大的韧性和综合竞争力，实现了快速回稳。与此同时，贸易结构不断优化，机电产品、高新技术产品成为出口主体，民营企业成为对外贸易主力军。引进外资和对外投资发展成果显著，2022年实际使用外资以人民币计首次突破1.2万亿元。按可比口径同比增长6.3%。以美元计达到了1891.3亿美元，增长8%，引资规模依然保持世界前列。与此同时，从正面清单到负面清单管理，从"外资三法"到《外商投资法》，我国开放的大门越开越大，正在成为众多外商投资的热土。

三、长三角一体化层面

2022年是长三角一体化上升为国家战略的第4年。长三角地区以4%的国土面积创造了全国1/4的经济总量，是我国经济发展最活跃、开放程度最高、创新能力最强的区域之一。过去4年，沪苏浙皖大动作频频，各扬所长、协同发力，紧扣"一体化"和"高质量"两个关键，打造强劲活跃增长极，产业集群加速崛起，一体化示范区建设硕果累累。

长三角加快推进经济高质量发展进程。截至2022年8月，上海、宁波、苏州的专精特新企业数量分别位居全国第2、4、10位，主要行业聚焦通用设备制造、电子信息制造、软件信息服务、生物医药、高端装备制造等领域，形成了相对稳定的产业链上下游合作关系，专精特新企业对于提升区域制造业发展水平、增强产业链供应链韧性发挥着积极作用。当下，为破解供应链安全等问题，长三角部分企业正筹谋在大区内推行"业务多地化布局策略"，积极寻找"中国+1"或"中国+2"的业务备份中心。长三角城市应对的复杂外部环境是共通的，需全力发挥整体优势，让产业链齿轮精准咬合，构建长三角共同市场，做足内需为主导、内部可循环的文章，携手打造改革开放新高地。

"十四五"规划勾勒一体化发展图景。《长三角一体化发展规划"十四五"实施方案》明确了22项重大政策、104个重大事项和16类重大项目，提出到2025年，长三角一体化发展取得实质性进展，一体化发展的体制机制全面建立，跨界区域、城市乡村等重点区域板块一体化发展达到较高水平，科创产业、协同开放、基础设施、生态环境、公共服务等领域基本实现一体化。从率先构建新发展格局、推进重点区域联动发展、加快构建协同创新产业体系、推进更高水平协同开放、加强基础设施互联互通、共同建设绿色美丽长三角、共享更高品质公共服务、创新一体化发展体制机制、高水平建设安全长三角和保障措施等方面进行了详细规划，并提出发挥新媒体作用、统筹融媒体资源、讲好"长三角故事"。

四、上海市层面

党的十八大以来，上海市坚持扩大开放不动摇，以落实国家重大战略任务为牵引，形成了一大批首创性改革、引领性开放、开拓性创新，已经成为全方位高水平对外开放高地。积极实施扩大内需战略，促进消费提质扩容，社会消费品零售总额翻了一番，规模跃居全国城市首位。发挥市场在资源配置中的决定性作用，促进商品要素资源在更大范围内畅通流动，百亿级千亿级商品交易平台数量倍增，现代商贸流通体系建设取得重要突破。同时持续推进贸易高质量发展，贸易枢纽功能不断增强，全球市场份额持续提高，跃升为全球最大的贸易口岸城市。

虹桥国际中央商务区（简称"商务区"）聚焦持续推动经济高质量发展，总部型经济加快集聚，高附加值、高成长性、高能级产业集群加速形成，流量型经济稳健发展。"一核"动力更加强劲，"两带"建设亮点纷呈。"虹桥功能"服务新发展格局，大交通、大会展、大商务三大核心功能不断凸显，国际定位进一步强化，全球资源配置能力显著增强。"虹桥速度"引领高质量发展，商务区作为虹桥国际开放枢纽的核心承载区，2022年一季度税收收入同比增长20.9%，快于全市平均增速10.7个百分点；商务区2022年累计吸引投资和开工建设项目总额近1 200亿元，相比2021年增长60%。"虹桥担当"助力打赢大上海保卫战，在本轮疫情大考中，"大虹桥"强化水陆空协同联动，虹桥机场和虹桥火车站全力服务援沪"大部队"，国家会展中心"四叶草"成为方舱主力军，充分发挥了枢纽联通功能和资源配置能力。同时，"大虹桥"六个区统筹疫情防控和经济社会发展，有序推进复工复产，迅速落实助企纾困政策，为加快经济恢复重振打下坚实基础。

未来5年是全面建设社会主义现代化国家开局起步的关键时期，主要目标任务之一就是基本形成更高水平开放型经济新体制。作为虹桥国际开放枢纽区域功能布局的核心，未来5年也是这片151.4平方千米区域奋力打造国际一流中央商务区核心功能的关键窗口期。商务区将更好发挥地理和区位优势，打造国际化的营商环境，提升政府公共服务综合能力，承担更高水平开放的使命，形成具有相对独立功能的城市形态，更好地承载总部经济和流量经济。

第二节　经济运行

2022年，商务区克服疫情带来的巨大冲击，区域经济呈现稳定发展态势。2022年1—12月，商务区实现税收收入309.84亿元，剔除留抵退税因素后实现税收收入398.71亿元，同比增长15.2%。实现规上工业总产值484.87亿元，固定资产投资497.46亿元，社会消费品零售额523.58亿元。实现进出口商品总额616.59亿元，同比增长8.6%，外商投资合同金额23.06亿美元，外商投资实际到位金额10.86亿美元。新增法人企业数9 804家，累计达到61 459家。

一、招商引资取得实效

2022年，商务区精准发力形成招商引资新局面。进一步深化"1+1+4+X"联合招商工作体系，全面实施"虹桥国际商务伙伴计划"，推动虹桥品汇引进进宝汇并入选首批上海市直播电商基地，开展"全球购"虹桥消费系列活动，打造西片国际消费集群区，推动区域经济跑出加速度。会同四区积极走出去招商，先后到合肥、杭州、南京和太原等地举办长三角以及内资企业家圆桌会，形成招商热度和投资氛围。2022年，实现固定资产投资497.46亿元，引进投资类公司12家，总计划投资规模约800亿元。

表 1-1　2022 年虹桥国际中央商务区固定资产投资额　　单位：亿元

区　域	2021 年	2022 年	绝对增加值	增幅（%）
商务区	511.55	497.46	−14.09	−2.8
南虹桥片区	119.30	127.49	8.19	6.9
东虹桥片区	85.65	98.58	12.93	15.1
西虹桥片区	237.30	210.39	−26.91	−11.3
北虹桥片区	69.30	61.00	−8.30	−12.0

开放经济亮点突出，外资信心持续提振。1—12月，商务区外商投资合同金额23.06亿美元，外商投资实际到位金额10.86亿美元，同比增长100.0%，高于全市平均93.5个百分点。

二、消费市场不断回暖

2022年，商务区持续放大进博会溢出效应，进一步打响"虹桥品牌"。持续做大做强"6+365"常年展销平台，推动展品变商品、展商变投资商。持续提升虹桥进口商品展示交易中心、虹桥海外贸易中心、新虹桥国际医学中心等平台能级，大力支持虹桥品汇、绿地全球商品贸易港发展，并在30个城市分中心的基础上，不断扩大溢出规模效应，以更高水平开放促发展、促合作、促共赢，把进博会打造成为推动国内国际双循环相互促进的重要纽带、参与全球产业链供应链价值链的重要平台。1—12月，商务区实现社会消费品零售额523.58亿元，同比下降2.1%，增速高于全市平均7个百分点，恢复至2021年同期的97.9%，降幅较上半年和前三季度分别收窄11.8个百分点和1.2个百分点。商品销售额4 056.12亿元，同比下降11.5%，低于全市平均4.4个百分点，恢复至2021年同期的88.5%，降幅较上半年和前三季度分别收窄6.4个百分点和1.3个百分点。

表1-2　2022年虹桥国际中央商务区消费市场情况　　　　　　　单位：亿元

区 域	社会消费品零售额			商品销售额		
	2021年	2022年	增幅（%）	2021年	2022年	增幅（%）
商务区	534.62	523.58	−2.1%	4 582.19	4 056.12	−11.5%
南虹桥片区	269.18	271.69	0.9%	1 770.92	1 519.30	−14.2%
东虹桥片区	83.60	73.30	−12.3%	2 004.30	1 869.20	−6.7%
西虹桥片区	87.54	101.69	16.2%	521.47	428.72	−17.8%
北虹桥片区	94.30	76.90	−18.5%	285.50	238.90	−16.3%

三、国际贸易增长明显

商务区连续两年在虹桥国际经济论坛上举办"虹桥HUB大会"，推动虹桥海外贸易中心联系超过150个国家、地区和36家境内外商（协）会入驻，绿地全球商品贸易港设立61个国家馆和180家企业以及组织入驻,初步形成全球化贸易投资服务网络,进博会"6天+365天"一站式交易服务平台溢出带动效应持续放大。引进进宝汇直播跨境电商基地,推动虹桥品汇入选首批上海市直播电商基地,开展"全球购"虹桥消费系列活动,推动万科天空之城广场百余家品牌门店全面开店,进一步做强区域经济发展载体,形成数字新经济、低碳新能源、生命新科技、汽车新势力、品牌新消费等产业集群。在疫情的冲击下,2022年商务区实现进出口商品总额616.59亿元,同比增长8.6%,高于全市平均5.4个百分点。其中,进口商品总额448.95亿元,同比增长5%,高于全市平均5.5个百分点;出口商品总额167.64亿元,同比增长19.3%,高于全市平均10.3个百分点。

表1-3 2022年虹桥国际中央商务区进出口总额　　　　单位:亿元

	进口商品总额		出口商品总额		进出口商品总额	
	总额	增幅	总额	增幅	总额	增幅
商务区	448.95	5%	167.64	19.3%	616.59	8.6%

四、企业主体持续增加

2022年,商务区企业主体持续增加,新增法人企业数9 804家,其中内资9 626家,外资178家。截至2022年底,累计法人企业数61 459家,其中内资58 525家,外资2 934家。四上法人企业数2 048家,其中规上工业企业数191家。

与此同时,商务区加快集聚总部经济能级规模。大力推进国家进口贸易促进创新示范区建设,用足用好民营企业总部和贸易型总部政策,提升总部经济对商务区的贡献度。截至2022年底,累计吸引总部类企业500多家,其中经市级认定跨国公司总部企业44家、外资研发中心11家、民营企业总部44家、贸易型总部13家,形成以联合利华、中电投、波司登、安踏、携程等为代表的外资总部、央企二总部、长三角企业总部、民企总部和贸易型总部生态圈。南虹桥片区初步形成总部经济集聚,汇聚红星美凯龙等具有总部功能企业222家,推动恒力总部项目顺利开工;东虹桥片区积极实施"总部增能"计划,打造全球航空企业总部基地,入驻各类总部企业41家,航空经济、互联网经济、总部经济三大高地态势渐显;西虹桥片区着力打造长三角民营总部聚集区,吸引一批新兴科技总部,片区集聚各类总部80家,会展服务产业生态初具规模;

北虹桥片区新引进总部项目15个，完成年计划的150%，高标准推进虹桥新慧总部湾建设，储备一批优质研发总部项目，创新创业功能初步显现。

表 1-4　2022 年虹桥国际中央商务区法人企业数　　　　　　　　　单位：户

区　域	2022 年新增法人企业数			截至 2022 年底累计法人企业数		
	内资	外资	合计	内资	外资	合计
商务区	9 626	178	9 804	58 525	2 934	61 459
南虹桥片区	2 873	95	2 968	20 911	1 020	21 931
东虹桥片区	941	50	991	8 539	1 239	9 778
西虹桥片区	1 411	21	1 432	9 343	348	9 691
北虹桥片区	4 401	12	4 413	19 732	327	20 059

第三节　招商引资

一、组织开展投资虹桥招商引资系列活动

2021年下半年以来，商务区通过三个一批集中签约、企业家早餐会、"潮涌浦江　投资虹桥"等大型活动，形成招商引资热潮。2022年上半年疫情防控期间，商务区招商不停、洽谈不停、推介不停，通过线上形式举办一系列招商会，并召开分行业企业座谈会，积极帮助企业解决运营困难，强化以商引商作用的发挥。

围绕"潮涌浦江"投资上海全球分享季等主题，不断扩大招商引资朋友圈，与商协会、专业机构、国际商务伙伴开展合作，通过线上线下相结合的方式，累计开展活动30余场（其中开展线上活动18场，累计吸引线上参会人数达31万人次），相继举办"潮涌浦江　云聚虹桥"——虹桥国际中央商务区发展机遇说明会暨国际贸易新形势与企业应对、"潮涌浦江　云聚虹桥"——虹桥国际中央商务区发展机遇说明会（瑞士专场）等投促推介活动，"潮涌浦江　投资虹桥"——"资管大变局　存量新思路"

图1-1　虹桥国际中央商务区发展机遇说明会

共话资管机遇论坛、2022第十届中国汽车与环境创新论坛暨第十四届全球汽车产业峰会等主题峰会论坛，RCEP企业服务专场（抢抓机遇　用好RCEP生效红利）、FIEs Community @ Hongqiao 数字经济规则和外商投资企业发展机遇等企业发展讲座等，涵盖金融、产业、实物互联网、国际贸易、外商投资等多个领域，广泛凝聚国际商务伙伴合作共识，全力构筑虹桥国际中央商务区新一轮发展优势。

跟踪对接重点项目200余个，形成了以万生华态、百秋尚美等为代表的数字新经济集群；以天合光能、晶科能源等为代表的低碳新能源集群；以东软医疗、信达生物等为代表的生命新科技集群；以博世、米其林等为代表的汽车新势力集群；以锅圈、虎头局等为代表的品牌新消费集群，打造万商云集、要素汇集、多元交集的良好营商局面，进一步打响虹桥整体品牌。

二、精心实施虹桥国际商务伙伴计划

为加快推进虹桥国际开放枢纽建设，加大商务区整体推介，在国家战略和加快经济恢复政策叠加赋能虹桥国际中央商务区的窗口期，2022年9月14日，商务区举办了"潮涌浦江　投资虹桥"——虹桥国际商务伙伴计划启航活动。市委常委、常务副市长吴清，副市长宗明，市政府副秘书长顾洪辉，市政府副秘书长华源等相关领导以及企

图1-2　虹桥国际商务伙伴计划启航仪式

业代表出席活动。活动上，商务区管委会党组书记、常务副主任鲍炳章做"潮涌浦江共享机遇，投资虹桥共创未来"主旨推介，市商务委主任顾军发布虹桥贸易型总部和民营总部政策，市经信委总工程师张宏韬发布《虹桥国际中央商务区产业发展规划》，闵行区区长陈华文发布虹桥前湾发展规划，市政府副秘书长顾洪辉和市政府副秘书长华源共同启动虹桥在线新经济生态园，副市长宗明为新认定总部企业代表颁证，市委常委、常务副市长吴清为虹桥国际商务伙伴计划推杆启航。

　　商务区将以"潮涌浦江"系列活动为契机，精心实施虹桥国际商务伙伴计划，围绕国际专业服务、国际商贸促进、国际金融投资、国际产业集聚四个方面，与毕马威、万宝盛华等36家国际化、高能级知名企业（协会）建立长期稳定的伙伴关系，协同发展、合作共赢，加快培育壮大发展新动能，全力构筑未来发展新优势。

三、用好深化"1+1+4+X"招商联动模式

　　为放大虹桥国际中央商务区作为长三角强劲活跃增长极的"极中极"和联通国际国内的"彩虹桥"功能，进一步打响"虹桥机遇"品牌，以商务区联通国际的功能优势助力长三角企业国际化发展。

　　2022年9月以来，由虹桥国际中央商务区管理委员会（简称"商务区管委会"）牵

图1-3　长三角企业家圆桌会

头，联动闵行区、长宁区、青浦区、嘉定区政府和上海地产虹桥建设投资（集团）有限公司，充分发挥"1+1+4+X"招商联动机制，创新展开区域联动合作"走出去"推介调研新模式，赴合肥、杭州和南京等地，成功举办"协同发展、共创未来"——长三角企业家圆桌会，累计吸引长三角超百家企业参会。

商务区管委会党组书记、常务副主任鲍炳章做主旨发言，商务区管委会副主任孔福安做主题推介，各区领导做专题发言，并邀请中国银行、建设银行、交通银行、安永、万宝盛华、毕马威等专业服务机构专家为参会企业带来国际化发展课题分享。与会企业在会上进行了充分交流互动，纷纷对来商务区发展表示出浓厚的兴趣。推介活动意在充分发挥虹桥在企业国际化发展的综合赋能作用，聚焦长三角有国际化发展需求的民营企业"走出去"，并立足商务区进一步转型升级、创新发展。

第四节　虹桥效应

商务区积极构建"大宣传"的新格局，持续开拓创新，开阔国际视野，进一步加强协作配合，紧紧围绕重点工作，借助活动和平台，不断拓展信息素材来源，深度挖掘新闻线索，凝聚起做好信息和宣传工作的强大合力，有效促进招商引资、以商引商氛围的营造，在更广舞台推广大虹桥品牌。

做好商务区新年企业家座谈会系列宣传工作。2022年1月4日，商务区召开新年企业家座谈会，会前在元旦期间积极筹备邀请相关媒体参会，提供座谈活动相关企业背景资料和热点新闻素材，经统计，共有1家电台、3家报社、11家客户端、2家网站对此次会议进行报道，活动3日内累计阅读量达到67.2万次。

多角度策划一周年活动宣传方案。集结团队合力，紧密结合活动前、中、后三个阶段，打造立体化宣传效果。活动前期做好充分预热工作，同时根据各媒体个性化采访需求，做好相应采访安排及企业对接工作；一周年活动当天，配合现场会媒体对接及报道工作，做好发布会宣传报道，对接媒体，准备宣传报道素材；后期持续跟踪媒体报道，做好"二次宣传"和报道汇总统计工作。截至3月1日活动当天中午，主流媒体关于虹桥国际开放枢纽建设和商务区的相关报道和视频达到36篇（条）。

积极做好"潮涌浦江　投资虹桥"活动宣传工作。精心策划活动宣传方案，紧密围绕活动前、中、后三个阶段，组织媒体专题采访，安排现场宣传，组织专题采访，制作宣传视频，营造火热招商引资氛围。活动当天，吸引央视新闻、新华社、《人民日报》等20多家包括中央级媒体、市级媒体在内的各级媒体积极报道。会后跟踪相关报道情况，截至9月17日13时，据不完全统计，至少有1家电视台、1家广播电台、3家报社、5家中央客户端、10家本市媒体客户端，围绕"虹桥国际商务伙伴计划"和"投资虹桥"等关键主题进行报道，累计30篇，央媒相关报道浏览总量超65万次。东方网等媒体连发多篇文章，对此次活动进行持续报道，并在头条号、澎湃号等多渠道分发，累计阅读量超过145.5万次。

精心策划虹桥HUB大会，做好开场片制作、重点嘉宾和学者邀请、海报设计、重点媒体报道等工作，形成宣传热度和持续关注。论坛的高质量举办，立刻引来各方关注，包括央视《新闻联播》、《朝闻天下》、《人民日报》、新华社、《央广新闻》、中新社、《经济日报》、《中国经济导报》、《中国日报》、《小康》杂志等多家中央媒体都对本次论坛进行了不同形式、不同角度的报道。此外，上海发布、东方卫视、上海电视台、《解放日报》、《文汇报》、《新民晚报》、《青年报》、《新闻晨报》、上海人民广播电台、上海教育电视台、看看新闻、阿基米德、澎湃新闻、第一财经、东方网、上观新闻、新民网、界面新闻、周到上海等上海主流媒体纷纷报道了论坛的相关信息。第一财经和东方网设置了专题发布论坛的重要动态。

做好央媒等重点媒体的对接和联动。充分利用主流媒体的传播效率和能级，抢抓宣传阵地，讲好虹桥故事。结合一周年活动契机，中央电视台安排2次专访，主要针对商务区内万华生态、广联达、企业展示中心、企业服务中心等；《人民日报》、人民网分别发文1篇，新华社发文3篇；上海电视台新闻报道2条，上海广播电台报道4条；学习强国发文4篇；《解放日报》发文4篇；《文汇报》发文6篇。据不完全统计，关于虹桥国际开放枢纽和商务区的报道，累计总量近2 600条。央视财经频道计划推出《中国大区域》专题片献礼党的二十大，团队在收到采访函后，第一时间与节目组取得联系，召开专题视频会议。同时对接相关业务处室，进一步请教和确定拍摄对象。8月初全程陪同央视拍摄组踩点、拍摄、采访，做好服务和对接工作，成片于10月初在央视黄金时段播出。"潮涌浦江　投资虹桥"活动、虹桥HUB大会期间，积极对接央视新闻、《人民日报》等中央媒体，贯彻落实大宣传原则，提高活动曝光度，同步安排央媒专版重点报道相关活动。协调人民日报社记者专访商务区，于9月14日《人民日报》正刊经济版头条刊发商务区企业的专访报道。

第二章　虹桥国际开放枢纽建设

《总体方案》发布以来，按照市委、市政府工作部署，在市协调推进机制指导下，商务区全面推进《总体方案》29项政策措施（已落地26项），有效释放政策活力，提升整体区域发展的综合竞争力。同时在《总体方案》政策助力推动下，商务区作为"一核"取得良好发展势头，区域核心功能进一步增强，制度框架政策体系进一步完善，支撑联动服务长三角进一步强化。

第一节　顶层设计

商务区牢牢把握重大机遇，强化顶层设计，为未来发展夯基垒台架梁立柱，围绕"一大平台、三大任务、四大功能、五型经济"等要求，面向全球、着眼未来，对标最高标准、最好水平，提出到2035年，地区生产总值力争从1 400亿元增长到6 000亿元，税收收入从346亿元增长到1 500亿元，力争达到2 000亿元；同时展望2050年，重点从规划体系、制度体系、产业体系等方面进行顶层设计，形成叠加效应，并逐步发挥促进经济发展作用。

一、组织编制商务区国土空间中近期规划

基于上述战略定位和目标愿景的思考，搭建了工作专班，启动商务区国土空间中近期规划编制工作，对未来规划方案和空间布局进行研究梳理。同时，锚定《长江三角洲区域一体化发展规划纲要》《总体方案》以及贯彻中央对上海的"三大任务""四大功能"等战略要求，充分发挥对内对外两个扇面的枢纽作用，进一步明确基于2035年和2050年两个节点的商务区发展规划，打造全域联动、组团发展的空间体系，强化

核心区及主城副中心的辐射带动效应，构建创新协同网络、公共交通网络、开放活力网络、蓝绿空间网络，形成功能完善、各具特色、互联互通的五大功能板块，实现一张蓝图管全域，为未来发展立下四梁八柱。

表 2-1　虹桥商务区国土空间中近期规划指标体系

类别	指标名称	基准年（2020）	2025 年	2030 年	2035 年	类型
城市综合体征	可承载人口规模（万人）	95.5	—	—	110	预期型
	建设用地总规模（平方千米）	112.5	113	116	117.5	约束型
	外籍人口占常住人口比例（%）	4	6	8	10	预期型
	高学历人口占常住人口比例（%）	31	40	50	55	预期型
开放枢纽功能	总部型企业数量	357	500家左右	800家左右	1 500家左右	预期型
	国际性组织（机构）占全市比重（%）	—	25	30	—	预期型
	国际性展览占比（%）	—	80左右	80左右	—	预期型
	国际性会议占全市比重（%）	—	25左右	30左右	—	预期型
	交通枢纽年客流总量（亿人次）	4.2（2019年）	4.7	5.5	6.2	预期型
	新增外资法人企业数	—	1 500左右	3 000左右	—	预期型
品质城区建设	河湖水面率（%）	6.3	6.34	6.38	6.41	约束型
	森林覆盖率（%）	17	19	21	23	约束型
	人均公园绿地面积（人/平方米）	7.45	9.5	11.5	13.4	约束型
	骨干绿道总长度（千米）	—	60	120	180	约束型

续 表

类别	指标名称	基准年（2020）	2025 年	2030 年	2035 年	类型
品质城区建设	400平方米以上绿地广场等公共开放空间5分钟步行可达覆盖率（%）	88	90	93	95	约束型
	绿色交通出行比例（%）	68	70	80	85	预期型
	全路网密度（千米/平方千米）	4.8	5.5	7左右	8	约束型
	轨道交通站点600米用地（城市开发边界内扣除机场用地）覆盖率（%）	17.0/18.5（含局域线）	18.5/34.0（含局域线）	32.0/55.0（含局域线）	38.0/57.0（含局域线）	预期型
	新增住房中政府、机构和企业持有的租赁性住房比例	—	1月3日	1月3日	1月3日	约束型
	卫生、养老、教育、文化体育等社区公共服务设施15分钟步行可达覆盖率（%）	66	85	90	95	约束型
	绿色建筑星级运行标识认证面积（平方米）	—	300万	—	—	预期型

注：指标"可承载人口规模（万人）"的基准年数值为现状常住人口规模。

二、推动制定促进虹桥国际中央商务区发展条例

商务区经过十多年开发建设，已从形态开发进入开发建设与功能打造并重的阶段，多重国家战略赋能叠加，迫切需要制定相关地方性法规。通过立法的形式明确商务区功能定位、推进机制和制度体系，为商务区发展提供法制保障，在更深层次、更宽领域，以更大力度推进开放合作。2021年，虹桥立法列入上海市人大重点立法调研项目，商务区管委会成立课题组，2022年又深入各片区单位、企业园区一线开展专题调研，广泛听取政策诉求和意见建议，反复研究论证和修改完善，市人大财经委、常委会法工委等给予了全面指导，形成《上海市促进虹桥国际中央商务区发展条例》（初稿，简称《条例》），明确商务区的功能定位、推进机制和制度体系，把政策

固化为法律，在法治的前提下推进改革和制度创新，为商务区依法行政提供直接的法律依据。2022年1月，《虹桥商务区管理条例立法研究》被市委全面依法治市委员会办公室评为"二等奖"。

这项工作也得到市委、市人大、市政府高度重视。时任上海市委书记李强全力支持，龚正市长、蒋卓庆主任先后召开专题会议，研究《条例》立法工作，并对草案重要条款作出明确指示。10月28日，《条例》经上海市人大常委会审议通过，并于11月1日起施行。《条例》共九章六十九条，分为总则、区域规划与布局、国际化商务服务、国际贸易中心新平台、综合交通枢纽、产城融合、服务长三角一体化发展、服务与保障和附则。其主要特点有四个方面：一是突出政治站位，以法治保障强化国家战略落地实施。二是突出功能打造，建设新时代改革开放的标志性区域。三是突出协同开放，助力构建国内国际双循环新发展格局。四是突出主体作用，优化体制机制形成工作合力。

三、编制产业规划引领"四高五新"产业加快集聚

聚焦具有良好发展基础和未来前景的高能级总部经济、高溢出会展经济、高流量贸易经济、高端化服务经济，布局打造数字新经济、生命新科技、低碳新能源、汽车新势力、时尚新消费五大新赛道，构建"四高五新"产业体系。结合商务区"十四五"规划，围绕上海"3+6"主导产业以及发展"五型经济"要求，编制《虹桥国际中央商务区产业发展规划》，提出到2025年，努力构建"四高五新"产业体系（即高能级总部经济、高溢出会展经济、高流量贸易经济、高端化服务经济；数字新经济、生命新科技、低碳新能源、汽车新势力、时尚新消费），定期滚动完善调整，争取到2025年，实现"4311"产业发展目标，未来将集中打造高流量贸易经济、高端化服务经济、数字新经济、时尚新消费四个千亿级产业生态集群；打造生命新科技、汽车新势力、低碳新能源三个500亿级产业；举办100场国际性会展，国际性展览占比超过80%，国际性会议占全市比重超过25%；集聚综合性总部和功能性总部企业数量达到1000家。产业规划明确产业发展目标和产业定位及重点领域，优化产业空间布局，开展配套政策研究，为"十四五"期间商务区产业发展、项目招商与落地提供指引。

此外，商务区还积极落地推进一批创新性政策措施。全面推动《总体方案》落地实施，出台推广一批实施细则和应用案例。全面贯彻市政府支持商务区进一步提升能

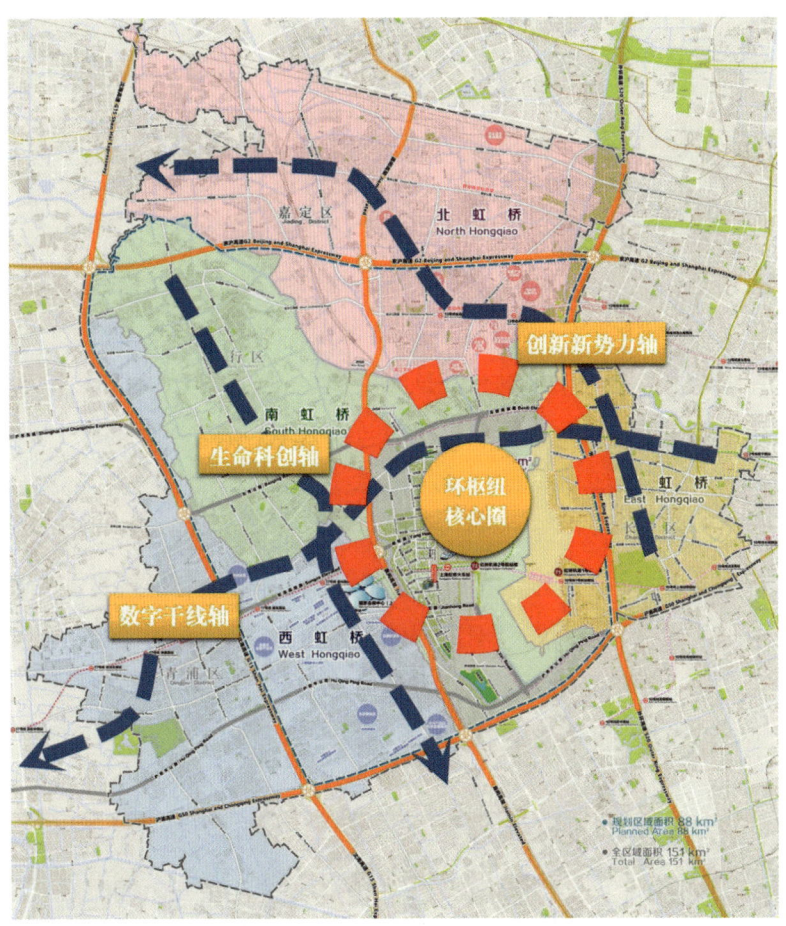

图 2-1　虹桥国际中央商务区"一圈、四片、三轴"

级的 23 项政策，制定实施促进贸易型总部和民营总部发展的鼓励政策，并会同市统计局和四区政府建立区域统计合作制度，引领支撑作用逐步显现。在市发展改革委牵头推动下，虹桥国际开放枢纽建设政策升级版正研究制定中，推动国家相关部门在"两周年"时出台一批高含金量、创新力度大的政策措施。

第二节　着力建设国际化中央商务区

紧扣"一体化"和"高质量"两个关键，加快推进高端商务、会展、交通功能深度融合，加快发展现代化服务业，建设高标准的国际化中央商务区。

夯实国际会展之都核心功能。依托国家会展中心，充分发挥上海市会展行业协会作用，搭建了虹桥国际会展产业园，已吸引包括云上会展、英富曼、中贸美凯龙等近200家会展产业链相关企业入驻。研究疫情防控常态下会展高质量发展路径，推进传统会展与数字会展有效结合。

打造进博会成果集中展示地。按照"政府引导、市场主体、政策支持、多方联动"原则，搭建一批面向"一带一路"国家和地区的商品直销平台、国别商品交易中心和专业贸易平台。推进虹桥品汇向线上平台和专业化交易平台发展，深化绿地全球商品贸易港国家馆特色和虹桥海外贸易中心分平台建设。

图2-2　虹桥品汇

　　打造"元气虹桥·全球GO"消费品牌，充分发挥进博会促消费稳增长作用，引导进博会溢出效应重点承接平台企业积极开展进博主题促销活动。如虹桥品汇开展推出咖啡文化周、国别缤纷月、清酒文化节等系列活动，打响"进口采购到虹桥、消费体验来品汇"品牌；绿地全球商品贸易港结合各国风土人情、艺术人文、美食佳酿等开展"G-Hub全球国别缤纷购"，全渠道推出万国啤酒节、中东异域商品展、土耳其当代摄影艺术展、卡洛芙珠宝节等线上线下互动体验活动；进宝汇通过"直播High购季"向全国消费者展示虹桥优质进口商品，增加线上目标消费群体对进博会和虹桥跨境商品资源的认知。

　　构建富有特色的现代服务业集聚区。拓展深化虹桥海外贸易中心平台功能。作为服务境外非政府组织服务的功能性平台，虹桥海外贸易中心新引进包括国际商事争端预防与解决组织、格鲁吉亚对外贸易联合会上海代表处、土耳其食品和饮料工业协会联盟上海代表处、香港中华工商总会上海代表处等5家重点机构，累计引进了新加坡企业中心、中国西班牙商会、香港中华工商总会等36家国际贸易投资促进机构，联系全球超过150多个国家和地区。新增虹桥海外贸易中心分平台，会同青浦区商务委、西虹桥等部门形成服务合力。2022年11月7日，中国食品土畜进出口商会主办进

图2-3　"元气虹桥·全球GO"购物节

图2-4　虹桥海外贸易中心

博会重要官方配套活动之一"中国进口食品行业峰会"，会上发布"上海虹桥·中国进口食品贸易指数"，为打造上海虹桥食品国际贸易信息中心地位，推动上海虹桥食品国际贸易集聚区建设奠定软实力基础。11月7日，新加坡中华总商会以"新格局、新机遇"为主题举办"新中商务论坛"，进一步促进新中两地企业交流互动。2022年，累计引进企业61家，服务境外企业2100余家，开展各类经贸活动300余场；成功推动大白兔奶糖、三牛食品、燕京啤酒等进入南非、肯尼亚、新西兰市场，实现双边共赢。

深化医药集聚区建设。2010年3月由上海市政府常务会议批准立项启动。整个园区占地100万平方米，其中一期42万平方米，二期约58万平方米。2017年6月，国家卫计委等5部委在全国遴选了13家国家健康旅游示范基地，新虹桥国际医学中心代表上海申报入选，成为国家级健康产业园区。园区一期地块上，复旦大学附属华山医院虹桥院区正式运营4年，业务量快速上升，2021年出院病人超过3万人次，其中来自长三角乃至全国其他省市的病人超过90%。园区一期还有7家高水平国际化医院（社会资本投资）和一个集约共享的医技中心大楼（包括影像中心、检验中心、药品供应中心等），总建筑面积70万平方米，医疗产业项目总投资超过130亿元。

图2-5　上海新虹桥国际医学中心

7家高水平国际化医院分别为泰和诚肿瘤医院、新加坡百汇医院、西南骨科医院、绿叶医疗美容医院、星晨儿童医院、慈弘妇产科医院和览海康复医院，这些医院和国外顶尖的医院以及本市优质的三甲医院通过各种形式进行品牌、技术、管理等合作。

园区二期已获批3家医院（绿叶利兰医院、协华脑科医院、圣康达医院）。除医院外，二期还将引进信达生物国际运营总部和全球研发中心、云南白药上海国际中心，聚焦大健康产业链上教育、研发、转化等特色项目。

第三节 着力构建国际贸易中心新平台

加速打造贸易型总部集聚新高地。出台了支持贸易型总部企业招才引智、加大对贸易型总部企业金融支持、支持贸易型总部企业提高资金运作和管理能力、支持贸易型总部提升贸易规模、支持贸易型总部企业拓展国际市场、完善贸易型总部企业服务机制等25条支持措施。首批认定贸易型总部30家，覆盖了新型跨境电商、离岸转手买卖、保税展示、保转跨、保转展、跨转保等多种贸易方式，国内批发零售类7家，国际货物贸易7家，国际服务与物流12家，平台交易4家，占比分别为23.3%、23.3%、40%和13.4%，排名前5位的国际贸易企业占比商务区进出口贸易额近23%。

加快打造长三角民营企业总部集聚区。设立商务区民营企业总部培育库，鼓励企业加快在商务区集聚业务、拓展功能，升级成为民营企业总部，在产业链、价值链、创新链上进行融合创新、发展壮大，加快打造长三角民营企业总部集聚区。

商务区汇集了海内外各类高端人才，特别是以商务区为"同心圆"吸引了大批跨城通勤的长三角"候鸟型人才"，近3年跨城通勤就业规模增长约47%。同时，为民营企业创造了大量投资契机。2022年，商务区累计吸引重点项目落地超800亿元，涉及72个民企投资类项目（其中近半数为长三角企业），总投资额450亿元，涵盖生物医药、数字科技、半导体、新能源等产业。在此基础上，商务区认定了2022年度34家民营企业总部，包括诸多高能级、新赛道领军企业，如美的上海总部、康德莱集团、华测导航，及知名消费品牌"唯品会""报喜鸟""美凯龙"等。

从企业投资规模来看，34家民营企业总部2021年度营业收入超500亿元人民币，纳税总额达22亿元人民币，占商务区总税收比重约6%；从企业产业布局来看，超七成企业与商务区"四高五新"产业体系高度匹配，包括以广联达、中颖电子、华测导航为代表的数字新经济，以康德莱、贝泰妮为代表的生命新科技，以重塑科技为代表的低碳新能源，以威马汽车、日泰汽车为代表的汽车新势力，以美的、波司登、唯品会、报喜鸟、美凯龙、迪桑特为代表的时尚新消费等，颇具特色的产业生态体系加快形成；从长三角协同发展来看，产业联动更加紧密，首批认定的企业中七成以上为长三角总部企业。

通过总部设在虹桥，分支机构与生产基地布局长三角，实现能级跃升；或是集团授权，管理和研发型总部入驻虹桥，接轨上海优势，"总部＋基地"的产业联动发展格局日益清晰，逐步成为总部企业发展的新路径。

推进全球数字贸易港率先成势。商务区是上海数字贸易发展的重点区域。2022年是《虹桥商务区全球数字贸易港建设三年行动计划》实施的第三年，按照打造联动全国、联通全球的数字贸易枢纽，搭建数字贸易企业成长中心、进博会溢出效应转化中心和长三角数字贸易促进中心的"一枢纽、三中心"框架，围绕跨境电商、数字内容、数字服务及行业应用和云服务，突出数字贸易服务功能集聚，商务区已集聚数字经济企业超7 000多家，其中具有相当规模企业2 200余家，涌现出以携程、爱奇艺、联影、华测导航、云上会展、东软、EDG、RNG等为代表的一批领军企业和独角兽企业；以百秋、容么么、仪菲、新易腾、锅圈、洋妆源、缙嘉科技等为代表的一批电商社交平

图2-6 代表性企业百秋集团

台企业；以斑马智行、芯易荟、万生华态、小i机器人、黑湖科技、涂鸦智能、震坤行、丹纳赫、迪普乐、联影、广联达、恒时计算机信息技术等为代表的一批数字内容和数字服务企业，聚焦会展、商务、旅游、物流、医疗、教育、文化、培训等行业应用，培育数字贸易新模式，在智能网联汽车、工业互联网、数字内容等领域形成产业发展集群。

深入推进全球数字贸易港承载平台建设，新增中国北斗产业技术创新虹桥基地为首批国家地理信息服务领域特色服务出口基地；新增虹桥品汇为首批上海直播电商基地；新增"虹桥之源"在线新经济生态园，携程智慧出行园、联合利华U创孵化器、行健SPACE孵化器等加速发展；国家对外文化贸易基地（上海）北虹桥创新中心引进数字文化及相关产业链企业近200家，产值超过5亿；虹桥进口商品展示交易中心、上海虹桥临空经济园区等市跨境电子商务示范区，上海虹桥临空经济园区、上海西虹桥商务开发有限公司—西虹桥商务区等市服务贸易促进示范基地，以及微软虹桥数字贸易产业创新赋能中心等功能显现。积极支持临空经济园区创建国家数字服务出口基地，推动国际互联网数据通道落地，探索高水平的跨境数据流动开放体系。

实施商务区在线新经济生态园规划建设。商务区围绕率先建成全球数字贸易港、创建国家数字服务出口基地目标任务，积极把握"大交通、大会展、大商务"三大核心功能与流量密切相关的优势，抢抓数字新生态、新业态发展趋势，积极布局和抢占数字化新赛道，与市经信委共同谋划"虹桥国际在线新经济生态园"建设，为区域发展持续注入新动能。

明确提出到2025年，在线新经济规模突破5 000亿元；引育50家以上头部企业和链主企业、200家成长型企业，集聚3 500家以上具有创新活力和潜力的在线新经济企业；推出50个以上应用示范场景；引入2家大所大院和2个联合实验室；基本建成长三角数字大脑框架的发展目标。

在线新经济生态园以"一核四区"组团式集群化协同发展为格局，总占地面积22.92平方千米，总规划空间载体面积约1 463.5万平方米，现可投入使用空间载体面积约1 099.8万平方米，重点聚焦数字贸易、数字会展、数字内容、数字健康、工业互联网、数字出行六大特色产业，探索抢抓元宇宙、量子信息、大数据、空天信息四大前沿产业，坚持产业数字化和数字产业化双轮驱动，做强特色，突破前沿，建设虹桥国际开放枢纽流量汇聚地，挖掘创造虹桥流量价值。

商务区管委会牵头抓总，在市经信委支持下，会同四区政府积极策划，先期安排了20个重点项目，涉及数字贸易、数字内容、数字健康、数字出行、工业互联网、元宇宙六大领域。在"潮涌浦江 投资虹桥"活动上，已由市领导宣布"虹桥国际在线新经济生态园"启动建设，并在市委、市政府关心支持下，"虹桥国际在线新经济生态园"被列入《上海市2022年政府工作报告》工作任务。

第四节 着力提高综合交通管理水平

遵循国际一流、枢纽引领、开放互联、绿色低碳、立体融合、一体布局、智慧互联、统筹协调的原则，聚焦枢纽、通道、网络和管理，提出"一主四辅的枢纽体系、五向辐射的联系通道、五个系统的区域网络、一体互联的综合平台"的商务区远期综合交通规划"1551"总体布局。

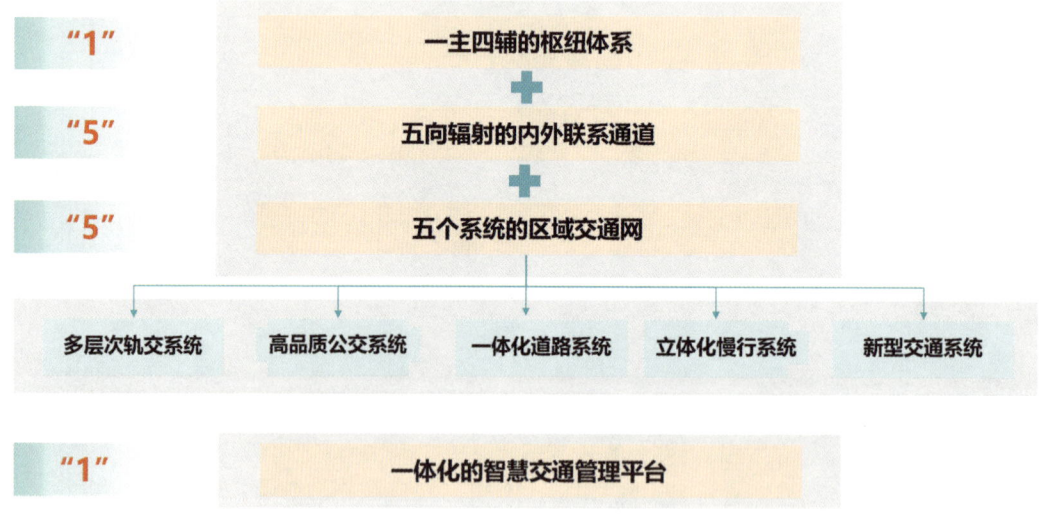

图2-7 远期"1551"总体方案布局

编制综合交通规划。为推动商务区的新一轮更高质量发展，配合《虹桥国际中央商务区国土空间中近期规划》，指导商务区综合交通的规划建设管理工作，商务区于2022年初启动《虹桥国际中央商务区综合交通专项规划》编制工作。

聚焦重要设施建设和核心区交通通达性与综合管理水平提升若干关键问题，明确了商务区综合交通的规划、建设和管理的目标，凸显了商务区"国际定位、开放优势、枢纽功能"的发展特色，体现了"高质量、一体化"城市发展的思路。

优化枢纽、通道、网络、平台综合交通体系。形成"一主四辅"的枢纽体系，实现辐射区域、链接国际能力提升。"一主"是虹桥综合交通枢纽，强化国际国内门户枢纽功能。"四辅"为四个地区级枢纽，兼顾长三角毗邻地区的城际服务。通过地区枢纽建设锚固市域铁路、城市轨交、公交、慢行等，实现轨道＋公交＋慢行的多网融合发展。

形成五向辐射的内外联系通道，通过干线铁路建设、市域铁路新建和高速公路完

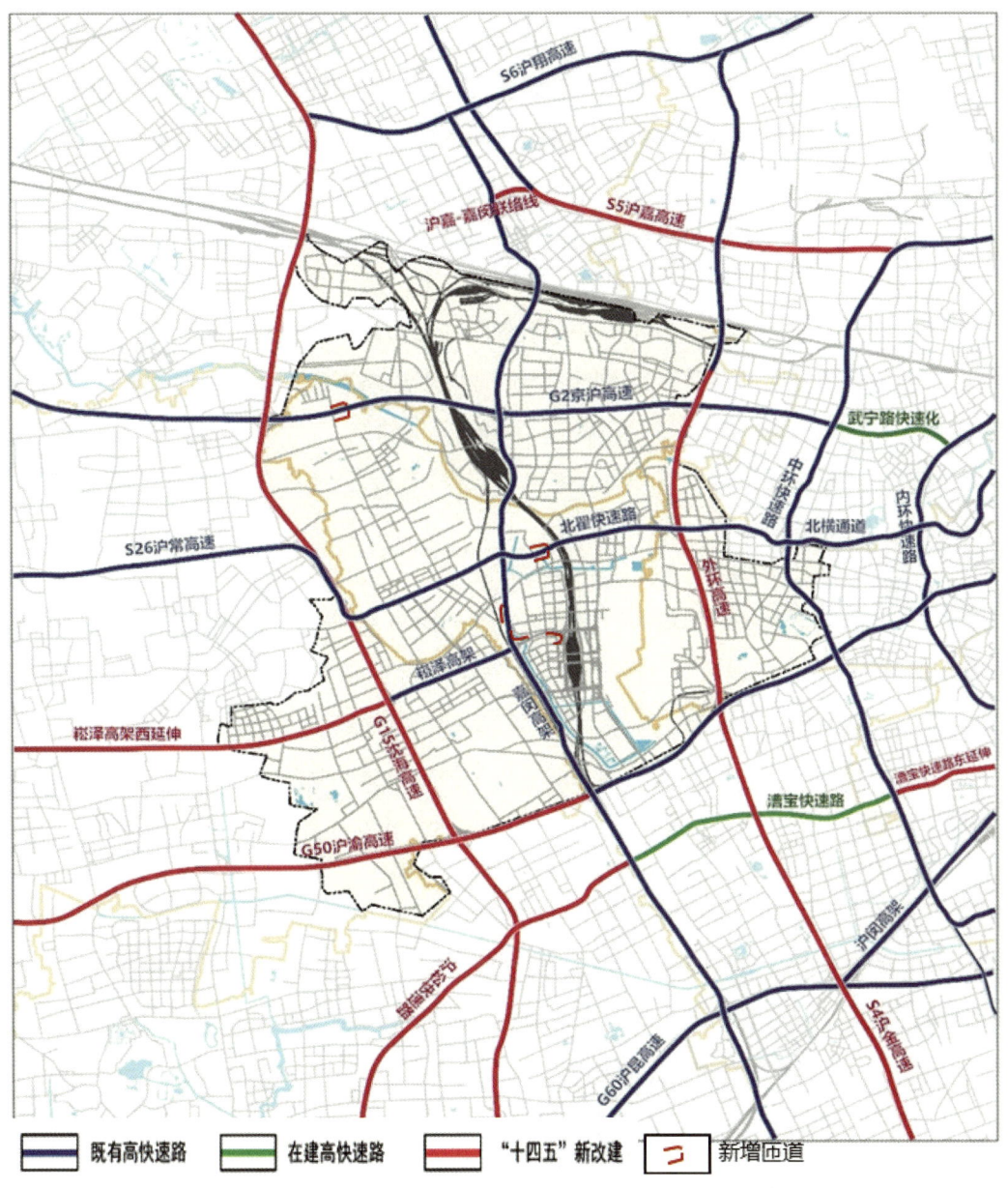

图2-8　商务区四横四纵高快速路

善，持续打造商务区与中心城区方向、浦东枢纽—临港新片区方向、长三角北向拓展带、南向拓展带和示范区方向等五个方向的辐射通道。形成五个系统的区域交通网络，创建国际一流商务区出行服务。形成构建一体互联综合交通管理系统，实现商务区管理的协同高效。

推进基础设施项目的前期研究和实施进度。商务区相关的交通设施项目中，沪苏湖铁路、沿江铁路等铁路干线已经开工，按计划于2024年建成通车。嘉闵线及其北延伸、机场联络线、上海示范区线以及轨道交通13号线西延伸、2号线西延伸等也分别于2022年7月开工，最迟于2028年建成。中运量公交71路西延伸也已经开工，计划2023年一季度建成通车。沪嘉高速—嘉闵高架联络线新建工程已于2022年10月开工。G15公路嘉金段（G1503公路—沪青平公路）改扩建工程，外环S20西段交通功能提升工程，G50沪渝高速拓宽改建工程等专项规划方案已公示。此外，申长路—金园一路工可已上报市发展改革委，正处于可评估阶段；申昆路—金运路工可已批复，计划年底开工。持续推进区区道路，完善四区内部地面干道路网进一步提升商务区的内外交通服务能力。

此外，商务区还持续推进综合交通设施建设，完善商务区综合交通体系，支撑国际开放枢纽基本建成。

立足新的目标愿景，重点规划方案包括：

一是形成一主四辅枢纽体系。通过建设芳乐路枢纽、金运路枢纽、淞虹路枢纽和会展中心枢纽四个地区级枢纽，形成一片一枢纽格局。强化虹桥综合交通枢纽的国际国内门户枢纽功能，提升商务区服务长三角和联通国际能级。

二是构建多层次轨道交通系统。远期规划形成涵盖8条城市轨道、4条市域铁路、1条既有铁路利用共13条线路约37个轨道站点（换乘站算1个）的多层次轨道交通系统，实现轨道站点600平方米面积覆盖率（35%—40%）。

三是建设高密度道路网系统。总体思路是形成"层次清晰、功能合理、高效畅达"的商务区高密度道路系统网络。目前"四横四纵"约85千米高快速路已基本建成，重点是通过优化高快速路在商务区的匝道布局，提升"四横四纵"高快速路对地区服务功能和构建"十横十纵"地面干道网。

四是规划高品质公交系统。总体思路是构筑大中运量公交为主体、常规公交为辅助、特色公交为补充的公共交通系统。重点是规划形成"核心放射＋切向加密"的多制式中运量公交网络通道和形成5条高频次骨干公交线路。

图2-9　虹桥枢纽

　　五是打造立体慢行系统。在核心区立体慢行网络的基础上，围绕15分钟生活圈，打造5个慢行示范区，同时，构建"九横九纵"自行车通道，满足部分自行车通勤出行需求和健身需求。

　　六是构筑一体互联综合交通管理系统。通过建设商务区一体化综合交通平台，实现数据共享、信息互通；实现会展、核心区、枢纽停车诱导与泊位共享的联动保障和商务区车流、人流系统智能导航。

第五节　着力提升服务长三角能力

辐射长三角一体化发展。与长三角区域主要城市基本实现了1小时通勤，民航、高铁、轨交体系等比较完备，形成独一无二的区位优势，为长三角区域商务贸易、人才流动、商品流通提供便捷的交通服务。支持长三角城市建设虹桥"会客厅"，比如江苏南京、苏州，以及浙江嘉兴、湖州等在商务区设立商办楼，全面展示推介各自特色、优势，为企业人才招引、科研孵化、市场推广等提供渠道，助力商务区成为长三角区域流量经济的交汇枢纽。

带动长三角协同开放。立足打造面向长三角、辐射全国、联通国际的法律服务"新平台"，建设集公共法律服务、专业法律服务、法治研究和交流等功能于一体的综合性国际中央法务区。支持本土企业拓展"一带一路"国家市场为重点，推动要素链接、产能链接、市场链接、规则链接，打造集信息、融资、人才、法律和风险防范等综合服务平台，以扩大对外开放来深化对内开放，加快打造国内大循环的中心节点、国内国际双循环的战略链接。

推动长三角协同改革。《总体方案》明确的设立长三角企业商标受理窗口、开展国际人才管理改革试点、设立跨区域社会组织等政策均已落地，已面向长三角跨省受理服务。构建虹桥国际服务商联盟，设立虹桥企业服务中心，为长三角企业提供商标注册和外国人工作许可受理服务，通过跨省政务服务平台，为企业办理设立、变更等事项35项，自助服务终端覆盖长三角39个县市。

服务长三角协同创新。强化"6+365"主平台建设，进一步发挥虹桥进口商品展示交易中心和绿地全球商品贸易港两大功能性平台功能，组织推进虹桥进口商品展示交易中心落户杭州、合肥、常州、黄山、嘉兴等地，进口商品集散地保税展示等功能逐步完善。依托虹桥—昆山—相城综合功能走廊，商务区与昆山加强进口贸易促进创新示范区联动。推动新虹桥国际医学中心医疗资源和技术共享，正成为长三角的"超级医院"。

加强"一核"与"两带"以及与长三角城市的交流互动，累计与24个长三角城市签署战略合作协议，推动商务区与长三角区域协同联动，健全完善上下游产业链，推

图2-10　虹桥国际中央商务区企业服务中心

动构筑"总部＋基地"产业集群。组织长三角民企总部集聚区推介暨项目签约大会，会同四区到长三角区域推介招商，先后到合肥、杭州等地举办长三角企业家圆桌会，逐步形成长三角企业到商务区投资氛围，实现协同发展、合作共赢。

成功举办虹桥国际开放枢纽建设工作现场会。会同市发展改革委以及相关区成立工作专班，聚焦核心功能、聚焦特色产业、聚焦重点企业，精心设计布展"企业展示中心"，高标准建设"企业服务大厅"和"人才港展示馆"，并推出一个高水平"现场展示点"，展示虹桥临空数字经济特色产业园内人工智能、数字健康、数字创意、数字出行四大产业生态，彰显商务区整体数字经济发展新动能，立体呈现商务区在虹桥国际开放枢纽国家战略实施一周年来的突出成效。

第三章 大上海保卫战

第一节 抗疫行动

商务区把疫情防控作为头等政治任务，在市委、市政府坚强领导下，积极会同市交通委、闵行区、枢纽运行管理单位，扎实开展枢纽疫情防控工作，守好安全底线，保障虹桥高铁站的平稳运行。同时抽调骨干力量，全力支援市级层面应急特需保障、市级方舱医院建设运营等工作，在打赢"大上海保卫战"中体现了虹桥商务区的担当作为。

兜住虹桥枢纽安全运行底线，守牢商务区抗疫红线。本轮疫情以来，市领导对虹桥交通枢纽运行与疫情防控高度重视。时任上海市委书记李强两次做出批示，上海市长龚正到虹桥站检查并提出要求，其他市领导先后到枢纽对运行秩序、大学生送站工作等检查指导。围绕"放外溢、防输入"的目标，管委会会同市交通委、闵行区政府及铁路、公安等相关单位成立工作专班，持续开展交通组织、疫情防控、滞留保障等工作。一是组织滞留人员进行核酸、抗原检测，做到"四应四尽"；二是严格分离旅客进出动线，开展到达层日常清场消杀；三是对进入车站的车辆及人员实施远端查验，符合离沪条件并持有当日车票的旅客方允许下车；四是为滞留人员发放食品、水等基本生活物资，设置临时安置点；五是每日对车站、街面、绿化带、高架路下等场所进行巡查；六是对滞留旅客进行分类安置，有序疏散，兜牢筑稳虹桥枢纽安全运行底线，维护了枢纽及周边秩序，为保障枢纽防疫、运行安全做出贡献。5月份累计安置滞留人员2万余人。为滞留人员搭建雨棚2 000多平方米，设置移动厕所16件和多处零食手机充电设施并每日发放物资，为打赢大上海保卫战做出了积极贡献。

全力支援特殊群体应急特需协调工作。联手相关企业和属地政府，搭建"特殊群体应急特需协调组"线上线下联动对接平台，通过饿了么、美团等"应急特需"专用

图3-1　抗疫工作专班

频道，及时解决老弱病残幼孕等特殊群体的生活物资和药品供应等方面的急难问题。累计收到应急特需工单44万余件，其中特殊人群应急特需求助工单28万余件，累计解决24万余件，解决率87%以上。

全力支援市级方舱建设运营工作。国展中心方舱的床位近5万个，高峰时日均转运8 000人左右，压力极大，不容有失。商务区管委会工作专班负责国展中心方舱医院出院转运等工作，3名同志在一线夜以继日、连续奋战50余天。全程挂图作战、预排方案、优化流程，实现由开始时从每天最高出舱1 000人左右，提高至每小时出仓2 000人以上，速度提升10余倍；缩短市民在停车场转乘区县车辆的时间，做到90%以上人员即下即上零等候。同时，针对方舱低龄儿童等特殊群体，形成工作机制，由专人单独照顾，并全程跟踪儿童安全回到家。

第二节　大走访大调研

按照"疫情要防住、经济要稳住、发展要安全"的要求，全面落实市委、市政府关于统筹疫情防控和经济社会发展各项工作部署，持续巩固疫情防控成果，推进国家、本市和商务区稳经济一揽子政策措施落实，深入开展领导干部大走访、大排查工作。

高度重视，压实责任。积极响应，制定方案，建立以主要领导任组长、分管领导任副组长、各业务处室负责人为成员的领导小组，根据区域实际情况结合工作分工，成立5个工作专班（分别为虹桥枢纽和地下空间，闵行、长宁、青浦、嘉定四片区），压实工作责任、明确任务分工，并召开部署动员会议，全面启动各项工作，确保干部真正走下去，情况真正摸上来，问题真正解决好。班子成员和处室领导干部迅速行动，发挥"1+1+4+X"联合工作体系优势，协调四个片区，全面排摸商务区范围内的代表企业和重要点位，提前排定走访排查计划，确保覆盖面的同时，防止重复走访。

形成合力，强化保障。跨前一步，主动作为，提前规划每周走访企业名录、走访时间等，做到心中有数。提前对接企业，了解企业的基本情况，以及初步了解受疫情影响企业当前阶段的困难等，针对相应的问题，提前做好功课，切实给出具体措施帮助企业解决难题。每次走访安排专员做好相关记录，对于内容较为复杂，涉及具体细节但确实比较重要，而现场又没有完整记录的，专员负责进一步对接企业联络人，翔实做好沟通对接。建立联络员制度、周例会制度，形成周计划、周总结、月度分析和信息快报制度，确保大走访大排查工作有序开展。通过走访把形势讲清楚、把政策落到位、把服务送上门，进一步增强市场主体和投资者信心。

注重实效，闭环管理。建立工作清单、问题清单，形成"大走访大排查问题及隐患处理情况表"，每两周进行一次综合汇总，对前期发现的问题和隐患做进一步跟踪反馈，形成现场排查、问题反馈和督促整改的工作闭环。针对走访中反映的各类问题、排查中发现的各类隐患，属于管委会职责范围的，要求各部门主动认领、从快从速处理，属于四区政府和虹桥枢纽各运营主体职责范围的，协调推动相关责任主体即知即办、立行立改。走访过程中，管委会坚持以倾听、调研企业发展诉求及招商引资建议意见为切入点，以全面促进区域经济高质量发展为重心，紧扣政策落实和经济发展两条工作主线，切实帮助企业解决了一批困难，提振发展信心。

形式多样，方法灵活。针对企业对惠企政策缺乏系统了解的问题，商务区管委会通过实地走访、现场座谈会和个别访谈等方式，全面向企业讲解商务区的区位优势、政策优势、人才优势、环境优势，并集中介绍商务区"十四五"规划建设愿景，让企业对未来在商务区发展抱有更大的信心。同时，针对企业提出的加大促消费资金支持力度，参与整体购物品牌打造的问题，商务区积极宣介商业体和企业复工复产政策，形成常态化解决方案。

在"防疫情"和"保平安"大排查方面，切实发挥好管委会的协调指导职责，督促属地政府和枢纽各运营单位落实主体责任，在发现问题、解决问题的过程中及时补好短板、堵塞漏洞、完善机制。一季度"促发展、保安全"大走访、大排查中，截至3月11日，商务区管委会累计走访企业211家，发现问题178个，全部办结；排查点位61个，发现隐患27个，全部整改完毕。6月启动的"防疫情、稳经济、保安全"大走访、大排查中，截至9月23日，累计走访企业434家，发现问题405个，已办结404个，正在办理1个；排查点位98个，发现隐患90个，已整改88个，形成处置预案2个。

第三节　纾企助力政策

为帮助受疫情影响严重的商务区企业加快恢复发展，推动区域开发建设、产业布局和功能集聚尽快回归常态水平，持续推进虹桥国际开放枢纽建设，主要从进一步发挥商务区专项资金扶持引导作用、积极推进金融政策落地两个方面开展相关工作：

充分发挥专项资金引导扶持作用。根据《上海市加快经济恢复和重振行动方案》要求，商务区研究制定了《关于充分发挥专项资金政策效益支持商务区受疫情影响严重企业加快恢复发展的工作方案》，明确为充分发挥商务区专项发展资金的引导扶持作用，帮助受疫情影响企业复工复产复市，对商务区范围内符合"四高五新"产业导向的企业（含功能性平台和特色产业园区（楼宇）运营主体）及贸易机构和社会组织符合以下条件之一的，商务区专项资金予以优先支持。同时，依据《上海市虹桥商务区专项发展资金管理办法》（沪财预【2019】15号）等有关规定，于6月初集中发布一批专项发展资金申报指南。

为帮助商务区企业更好地开展专项资金项目申报工作，商务区管委会于2022年6

表3-1　专项发展资金申报指南一览

序号	申　报　指　南
1	2022年度虹桥国际中央商务区支持现代服务业发展政策申报指南
2	2022年度虹桥国际中央商务区支持功能性平台发展政策申报指南
3	2022年度虹桥国际中央商务区支持打造虹桥进口商品集散地政策申报指南
4	2022年度虹桥国际中央商务区支持低碳实践区建设政策申报指南
5	2022年度虹桥国际中央商务区支持"智慧虹桥"建设政策申报指南
6	2022年度虹桥国际中央商务区关于支持内资总部企业发展的申报指南
7	上海虹桥商务区新型基础设施建设项目贴息申报指南

备注：《2022年度虹桥国际中央商务区关于支持贸易型总部企业发展的申报指南》于2022年8月发布。

月10日联合闵行、长宁、青浦、嘉定四区政府成功举办2022年上海虹桥商务区专项发展资金项目申报培训会。管委会相关业务处室、四区政府相关部门、商务区企业代表参会。

通过线上直播的方式，由商务区管委会相关业务处室进行专项资金政策宣贯，主要包括：推进低碳实践区建设、支持"智慧虹桥"建设、支持功能性平台发展、促进现代服务业发展、打造进口商品集散地、支持内资总部企业发展六大类项目申报指南。这次培训会反响热烈、效果显著，会前报名阶段即有150家企业报名，实时在线人数累计近500人。管委会也响应参会企业需要，通过建立专项资金项目申报咨询微信群，进一步为企业答疑解惑，加强沟通交流，帮助企业做好后续项目申报工作。

会同闵行、长宁、青浦、嘉定四区政府对2022年度申请虹桥商务区专项发展资金支持项目进行了评审和批复。为帮助企业解决资金压力，商务区管委会积极组织企业开展项目申报工作，按计划分2批申请市级财政资金拨付，对首批在6月完成评审批复的项目，商务区管委会立即组织向市财政局申请首批项目资金拨付，确保资金及时拨付至企业。2022年度累积批复项目124个，扶持总金额3.6亿元。结合2020—2022年已批复项目分年度资金需求，当年度实际补贴资金3.8亿元（其中：市级资金1.9亿元，区级资金1.9亿元）。

积极推进金融政策落地。支持企业开立自由贸易账户。支持商务区内通过自由贸易账户开展跨境交易本外币结算和境外融资业务。通过金融机构推荐，商务区定期向人民银行上海总部报送符合条件的企业名单的方式，形成常态化工作机制，已累计推荐172家企业开立自由贸易账户，多家企业已使用账户开展日常结算、结售汇及融资等相关业务，享受到了自由贸易账户结算汇兑的便利。

扩大离岸经贸企业"白名单"。进一步支持商务区内符合条件的企业积极开展离岸经贸业务，扩大离岸经贸企业"白名单"。2022年，商务区内累计已有12家企业纳入离岸经贸业务推荐企业名单。后续将继续鼓励商业银行提供基于自由贸易账户的跨境金融服务便利，优化非自由贸易账户离岸贸易资金结算等相关工作，全力推动金融政策制度创新落地，推进虹桥国际开放枢纽建设。

加强商务区特色金融服务。为贯彻落实《上海市加快经济恢复和重振行动方案》的要求，切实发挥金融服务实体经济的重要作用，商务区管委会分别于2022年6月13日、6月30日组织召开了2场稳外贸促发展金融纾困政策宣讲会，邀请来自工行、农行、中行、建行、交行、浦发银行、汇丰银行、上海市联合征信有限公司及中国出口信用保险公司等金融机构专家对在疫情期间推出的特色金融业务进行政策宣讲，如建行上海分行出台的全力抗疫情助企业促发展"十五条"、交行上海分行推出的"助力复工复产八项举措"等金融服务，为民助企、同心抗疫，助力企业渡过疫情难关。

完善现代服务业专项资金补贴政策。在制定商务区现代服务业申报指南政策中，首次将商圈促销和消费券发放等线上线下活动列入高端商务活动范围，加大对商圈或企业促消费活动的补贴力度，符合条件的可享受最高不超过100万元人民币的补贴，12家企业申报相关促消费活动补贴。同时，注重为商圈与银行搭建"桥梁"。帮助建设银行上海第三支行、中国银行虹桥商务区支行等商业银行与虹桥天地、龙湖天街等商圈对接，充分发挥各方的资金、平台、宣传等优势，打造商务区新一轮消费热点。与此同时，加快推进打响虹桥消费品牌专项任务。细化促进消费和经济恢复的方案，积极筹备"进口嗨购节""元气虹桥·全球GO"等活动，联合10余家商务区内商圈或平台，统筹整体活动安排。此外，加大品牌宣传，通过市级公共新闻媒体推动联合发文和新兴媒体平台高频分发等方式，提升商务区消费品牌影响力。

第四节　复工复产复市

自生产生活秩序恢复以来，第一时间出台商务区专项发展资金支持政策，实打实为企业纾困解难，全力推进商务区复工复商复市，保持经济发展工作"不断电"，商务区经济活力加速回归，各片区加快重点项目引进。

一、闵行片区复工复产复市

（一）新虹街道

街道共有入驻企业3 357家，企业员工56 390人，其中酒店宾馆12家、长租公寓2家。6月1日全面解封前，协助4家企业（其胜生物制剂、虹桥商务区新能源、震坤行工业超市、才烁人才服务）获得闵行区经委开具的商请函和"白名单"资格，帮助35家商超、11家餐饮店、6家药店、2家电商前沿站实现复工复产。

通过网络直播、企业走访、工作站日常对接等方式对政策进行大力宣传，新虹街道和南虹桥集团走访区域内2 700家企业，问困难、议发展、给政策，重点宣传落实加快经济恢复和重振的市50条和区18条政策。针对走访中企业反映较为集中的"流动资金不足"问题，统筹区域金融机构资源，成立金融行业党建联盟，搭建金融服务政策宣讲平台，促进银企信息互通、资源共享。

加快推动复工复产、复商复市。根据区相关文件要求，制定了《新虹街道关于持续巩固疫情防控成果　有序复工复产的实施方案》。成立了复工复产工作专班，明确了各自复工复产工作内容及流程。辖区两家大型超市线下营业有序进行，自5月18日开业至6月1日人流量达到2 500人，完成营业额118万元。

制定复工复产白名单企业清单。根据区经委下发的《推进本区重点商办楼宇有序复工的通知》，制定包含41家企业的明细清单。截至5月31日已完成商业体100%复工，亿元楼复工60%，并于5月31日进行一次商业体应急演练。

加快落实防疫责任体制。对名单内有复工意向的企业抓紧落实防疫主体责任制度，将企业防疫负责落实到个人。组织线上视频会议，向企业强调复工复产中需要做到的闭环管理、环境消杀、分区管理等各项工作，并让物业负责人针对园区内企业制定复工复产要求并审核相关人员及防控方案。

加快创建"无疫企业""无疫楼宇"。指导企业强化疫情防控不放松，管得好才能放得开；坚持分类分区管理，划小管理单元，科学开展核酸抗原筛查，哨点前移，快速发现、及时处置疫情；逐步推动商务区楼宇全面复工，扩大商业楼宇复工面，创建无疫企业、无疫楼宇，打通其和无疫小区之间的链接。

（二）华漕镇

华漕镇共有规上工业企业53家，规上商贸企业84家，规上营利性服务业企业44家，在上级部门的指导下，统筹考虑区域疫情和经济社会发展，逐步开展重点企业复工复产。在疫情封控期间，为保障各企业留守员工的基本生活，园区为企业留守人员订购保供套餐，尽全力解决留守员工的实际生活需求，得到了大家的一致认可。复工复产后，由于一些企业对防疫物资采购渠道不熟悉，园区物业公司及时协助企业采购抗原试剂、消毒水等防疫物资，解决了企业的燃眉之急。

早启动快节拍强宣传。利用原统计群和企业群，及早尽快地将复工复产相关条件、安排、流程和最新工作要求告知企业，先行排摸掌握企业复工时间安排，及时回应复工复产工作中企业和员工关切问题；制定《华漕镇关于持续巩固疫情防控成果 有序复工复产的实施方案》，明确相关部门职责和各阶段工作任务，下发给村居属地单位，统一认识，健全工作机制。

高效率高质量推复工。截至5月31日，共计审核重点企业复工申请59份，其中通过申请36份；审核"员工返岗车辆通行证""货物运输车辆通行证"等56批次，涉及车辆110辆；审核新增返岗人员"复工码"38份，涉及人员721名。针对樽轩、优乐加、一号商务地块等园区、商务楼宇物业管理方以及鸣志总部的复工方案，联系区疾控上门指导，根据场所实际，优化红、黄、蓝、绿四区设置，完善消杀方案。指导企业申请场所码，购买数字哨兵，协助企业建立核酸检测志愿者队伍，共有65名企业职工志愿者完成培训并取得证书。

强监管促整改保落实。建立全社会共同防控体系，落实"四方责任"，即属地、部门、单位、个人责任。复工前、中、后，组织镇领导、职能部门等对企业进行实地走访38次，了解企业需求及困难，给复工复产企业发放中药预防包1 850份。针对存在的疫情防范风险点，督促企业及时整改，并进行"回头看"，确保安全生产。

专人专管一企一方案。重点指导好企业做好复工复产疫情防控"一企业一方案"，做好场所分区分类管理、企业员工管理、物流管理和防疫物资管理、应急处置预案

图3-2　南虹桥复工复产

的制定和演练等。按照防疫相关要求，园区指导16家企业落实防疫专人专管，形成
"一企一方案"。及时检查企业防疫措施落实情况，如分区设置是否到位、是否张贴
明显标识、是否配置消毒用品等。遇到问题及时规范整改，为企业健康发展创造有利
条件。

二、长宁片区复工复产复市

疫情发生以来，区东虹办坚持"动态清零"总方针不动摇，按照"疫情要防住、
经济要稳住、发展要安全"的总体要求，推动"一街一镇一园区"进一步增强阵地意
识，压实"四方责任"，以坚决果断行动推动各项防控措施落地见效，坚决彻底拧紧疫
情传播的"水龙头"，持续加快社会面清零攻坚，全力以赴助力长宁区和全市打赢疫情
防控攻坚战。

（一）程家桥街道

全力以赴助力符合条件的企业复工复产，累计进入市级复工复产白名单的企业共
为13家。如中国航空油料有限责任公司华东分公司成为第一家疫情期间辖区驻守单位
翻牌进入白名单的企业，街道第一时间协助企业同投促办做好沟通，及时递交相关材

料，并在当天即完成审核反馈，最终企业获批进入市经信委第四批"白名单"，并于5月18日为第一批返岗人员（39人）申请复工码，5月24日为第二批返岗人员（237人）申请复工码，保障企业顺利实现了驻守人员的换岗、返岗。日通国际物流（中国）有限公司上海分公司作为一家从事空、海、陆、仓储等服务的综合性物流公司，随着客户逐步复产复工，原有驻守人员已无法满足业务需求，急需员工到外区仓库复工，街道在得知此情况后，及时对企业申请复工复产做出指导，最终企业获批进入市商务委重点外贸企业"白名单"。此外，针对前期暂时不具备复工条件的企业，街道也安排专人专班做好对接服务，最大程度保障企业基本运转。

（二）新泾镇

设置复工复产专班，以"楼宇园区群""重点企业群""沿街商铺群"全力助推重点企业和重点楼宇复工复产复市。依据楼宇园区群统计，10栋楼宇共326家企业复工复产，在岗人数3 380人，复工率97%。集体企业8家，在岗人员320人，百分之百复工复产。承租鑫达楼宇企业101家，复工率90%。持续强化政府管物业、物业管企业、企业管个人的三级责任体系建设，建立复工咨询登记备案小分队、复工专项消杀小分队、物资保障小分队，开设金融园核酸检测专场、设置楼宇核酸亭、牵线银行信贷云服务，坚持把服务送上门；汇总防疫物资购买渠道、提供白领午餐服务清单、公布社区疫情应急处置联系人，每天走访企业，以全方位支撑为楼宇园区企业复工复产保驾护航。建立"商街商圈攻坚组"，由镇领导班子带队不定期对沿街商铺开展飞行检查，巩固社会面防控成果。探索制度化"破题"方向，主动作为开展新泾镇"企心协力、疫路同行"专项行动。通过走访累计搜集各类企业诉求301条，咨询电话500余个，累计解决涉及企业复工复产、生活物资需求、防疫物资需求、惠企政策咨询等各类需求共计105条，聚焦重点企业，实现一对一式全方位服务。

（三）临空园区

加强分区分级差异化管控，针对园区留守人员，累计组织开展核酸检测8.5万人次、抗原检测16.4万人次，做到"应检尽检"。在保供保障方面，设立近800平方米物资中转站，向近6 000名留守人员发放7批次物资；协调35家重点企业的1 300余名员工纳入市级复工复产"白名单"率先返岗，解决人员释放、供应链疏通、政务服务、物资保障、政策落地等11大类145项企业诉求。园区12345市民服务热线累计受理群众诉求316件，接听求助电话700余个。在6月恢复正常生产生活秩序后，全面推动企业复工复产。开展清洁家园、守护家园、纾困解难"三大专项行动"，为园区企业复工复

图3-3　东虹桥复工复产

产提供保障。在园区范围全覆盖设置30个常态化核酸采样点，满足企业日常检测需求。园区181幢楼宇的1 500余家在地企业在6月底前基本实现全面复工复产。

三、青浦片区复工复产复市

徐泾镇（西虹桥公司）成立复工复产工作专班。4月23日，成立复工复产专班，通过一企一表工作制开展资料审核及现场检查，严格落实企业的防疫方案、防疫专班、隔离点设置、防疫物资储备、返岗人员管理等情况。5月，制定《虹桥国际中央商务区青浦片区复工复产工作方案》，并明确了分批复工名单。

开展包干式企业大走访。领导干部开展组团式走访企业，深入重点企业及急需纾困企业，建立了点对点"包干"制度，健全企业诉求快速回应和解决问题的服务机制。

用好政策鼓励支持措施。全力协助企业申请"虹桥国际中央商务区专项发展资金"，缙嘉科技、华测导航、威马汽车、中核同创等18家企业申报专项资金，总金额超1 241万元。积极帮助企业申请"青暖"22条政策及"张江国家自主创新示范区专项发

图3-4　西虹桥复工复产

展资金""困难行业稳岗补贴""防疫紧急纾困融资额度"等各项抗疫惠企政策，确保企业应享尽享、能用尽用，累计落实两批（产值）扶持资金140.4万元、国有房屋免租金170.3万。

用活金融工具。6月28日，青发集团与国家开发银行上海市分行牵头，会同区内13家金融机构，正式发放虹桥开放枢纽核心区域建设项目首笔贷款，为全力促进经济快速恢复和重振提供了有力保障。

持续推进商办项目建设，推动区域消费升级。9月30日，万科天空之城正式开业；蟠龙天地项目已接近尾声，预计明年上半年交付；联美首位等转型项目正在加速推进。

大力开展招商引资。积极参加2022上海全球投资促进大会暨"潮涌浦江"投资上海全球分享季、"潮涌浦江　投资虹桥"——虹桥国际商务伙伴计划启航等活动，青浦片区共有8个项目集中签约，项目总投资达到33亿元。举行了"世界会客厅　数贸新高地"——2022·虹桥徐泾数字经济园主旨论坛，搭建起政府与专家学者、企业等各方共谋青浦（徐泾）新时代发展路径的桥梁，聚势发展数字贸易和数字经济，着力打造"大商贸、大数字、大健康"三大产业集群。

四、嘉定片区复工复产复市

江桥镇持续放大29项政策、"20+3"条以及嘉定12条等政策叠加效应，发挥政策红利优势。服务精度不断提升，为持续放大虹桥、嘉定政策叠加效应，落实落细惠企政策，北虹桥不断提升服务能级，开展"一企一策"送政策上门服务，走访企业77户次，切实帮助企业解决实际困难。工作中预先全面掌握企业情况，量身打造所适配的政策组合包，以"一站式"服务标准做好全流程服务，大幅度提升企业的获得感和感受度。在专项资金使用方面，确保申报规范高效。截至12月，共计开展三批次专项资金申报评审工作，19个项目的资金合计3 803.085万元。项目数和资金额较2021年分别增长了约171%和209%，进一步提升了企业获得感。

图3-5　北虹桥复工复产

第四章　第五届中国国际进口博览会

第一节　基本概况

　　第五届中国国际进口博览会（简称"进博会"）是党的二十大后我国举办的首场重大国际展会。11月4日晚，在第五届进博会开幕式上，习近平主席在视频致辞中肯定了进博会的重要作用和丰硕成果，阐释了以中国新发展为世界提供新机遇的开放举措，强调中国将推动各国各方共享中国大市场、制度型开放、深化国际合作三个机遇，彰

图4-1　第五届进博会掠影（一）

显了中国同世界分享发展机遇的坚定决心，为进博会"越办越好"指明了方向。中共中央政治局常委李强在上海出席开幕式并致辞，国务院副总理胡春华、上海市委书记陈吉宁出席。

　　11月5日上午，"RCEP与更高水平开放"高层论坛举行，国务院副总理胡春华、上海市委书记陈吉宁出席并致辞。六天的时间里，开放合作的思想火花在虹桥国际经济论坛碰撞，全球领先的技术理念在展会亮相，各国企业共享进博新机遇、共享开放大市场，第五届进博会实现了安全、精彩、富有成效的预期目标。

　　第五届进博会共有145个国家、地区和国际组织参展。24场虹桥论坛活动顺利举办。来自127个国家和地区的2 800多家企业参加企业商业展；展示438项代表性首发新产品、新技术、新服务，超过上届水平。首次搭建的数字进博平台吸引368家技术装备企业线上参展，组织直播或转播活动64场，浏览量达60万次。坚持"政府+市场"发展方向，组建39个交易团、近600个交易分团，新增4个行业交易团、近百个行业交易分团。69个国家和国际组织亮相线上国家展，较上届增长13%。"中国这十年——对外开放成就展"综合展示区全方位、立体化展示新时代我国对外开放辉煌成就。进博文化展示中心全景展现5年来进博会发展历程和举办成效。专业配套活动和人文交流

图4-2　多个国家、地区和国际组织参加第五届进博会

活动内容丰富，精彩纷呈。现场服务保障不断优化完善，做好疫情防控工作。截至11月10日12时，累计进场46.1万人次。第五届进博会按一年计意向成交金额735.2亿美元，比上届增长3.9%。在各方共同努力下，第五届进博会实现了成功、精彩、富有成效的预期目标。

第五届进博会开幕式受到国际国内广泛关注。国家主席习近平在开幕式视频致辞中指出，中国将按照党的二十大部署，坚持对外开放的基本国策，坚定奉行互利共赢的开放战略，坚持经济全球化正确方向，推动各国各方共享中国大市场机遇、共享制度型开放机遇、共享深化国际合作机遇，为共创开放繁荣的美好未来注入强大正能量。中共中央政治局常委李强莅临会场致辞，并于开幕式前巡视企业展，同重点参展企业负责人集体合影。多国领导人和国际组织负责人以视频方式致辞。国务院副总理胡春华主持开幕式。来自82个国家、地区和国际组织的101位部长级以上嘉宾线上出席。

虹桥论坛凝聚开放共识。重点活动方面，"RCEP与更高水平开放"高层论坛围绕2022年生效的RCEP协定、区域经济一体化和更高水平开放等重要议题，邀请政商学研各界嘉宾参与讨论，为构建开放型世界经济贡献智慧。《世界开放报告2022》发布暨国际研讨会公布最新世界开放指数，深度挖掘开放规律，努力打造世界开放领域的"风向标"和"晴雨表"。发言嘉宾方面，24场活动共有385位嘉宾线上线下致辞或参与研讨，其中包括9位副国级以上政要、68位省部级以上政要、3位诺贝尔奖获得者、19位两院院士及社会科学院学部委员，以及其他知名专家学者和世界500强和行业龙头企业高管等。专业机构参与方面，9个中央部委、4个省市、3个专业智库合作主办专业领域分论坛；其间发布17个专业报告，打造"《世界开放报告2022》旗舰报告"+"专业领域品牌报告"+"分论坛合办单位专业报告"成果体系。国际组织参与方面，新增联合国工发组织、联合国人口基金、联合国全球契约组织、联合国减灾办、国际贸易中心、世界知识产权组织等6个国际组织主办分论坛，邀请更多国际嘉宾参与。

企业商业展质量更优。共有284家世界500强和行业龙头企业参展，数量超过上届，回头率近90%，展台特装比例达到96.1%，均高于上届水平。食品及农产品展区参与国别和企业来源最广、数量最多，共有104个国家的1 076家企业参展。汽车展区突出智能低碳，展示全球汽车工业最新发展成果。技术装备展区聚焦"双碳"、集成电路、人工智能等热点领域，集中展示前沿技术和高端装备。消费品展区发布众多首发展品，积极倡导绿色可持续生活方式。医疗器械及医药保健展区吸引全球十五大药品巨头、十大医疗器械企业参展，公共卫生防疫专区集约化展示国际先进公共卫生防疫成果。服务贸易展区汇聚39家世界500强和行业龙头企业，以及众多细分领域隐形冠军。创新孵化专区153家科技创新小微企业集中展示创新产品，评选活动获大量网民关注。

国家综合展打造沉浸式观展体验。作为进博会重要组成部分，国家展始终坚持全球公共产品属性，不断创新展览展示方式，吸引世界各国广泛参与。第五届线上国家展共有69个国家和国际组织亮相全新打造的数字展厅，各参展方借助沉浸式展示方式，全面展现其科技创新、文化艺术、投资环境等领域精彩内容，累计访问量5 900万次，超过上届。摩纳哥元首以及奥地利、尼泊尔、哥斯达黎加、冰岛、阿联酋、意大利等多国部长级官员、驻华大使和贸易促进机构负责人通过视频方式为国家展致辞，高度认可进博会推动各国各方共享发展机遇的作用。

专业配套活动质效提升。中央部委、地方政府和国际组织等共举办98场配套现场活动，涵盖政策解读、对接签约、产品展示、投资促进、研究发布等多个类别，活动质量和成效进一步提升。展中贸易投资对接会累计达成合作意向293项，意向签约总金额超59亿美元。组织82场集中签约活动，达成意向合作超过600项。组织专场线上对接活动，推动参展商和采购商开展云端交流、洽谈签约。开展94场新品发布活动，展示171项前沿科技产品。

人文交流活动丰富多彩。人文交流活动总展示面积增至3.2万平方米，为历届之最。意大利、中国香港特别行政区和30个省区市组织715家机构参与展示，参展单位数量较上届增长16%。239项非遗项目、275个老字号品牌以及10条全国示范步行街展示其特色内容。打造"人文街区"，已有10个省区市设置人文交流长期展厅，总面积逾1.2万平方米。多家艺术表演团体共呈现54台高水准文化公益演出，其中包括世界级非遗项目4个、国家级非遗项目9个，演出总场次达75场。中国香港地区的艺术团体首次登上进博人文舞台。

展会现场服务务实有效。优化"线上点餐，到店取餐"功能，增设就餐座椅，降低人群聚集风险。引入全球首创多工种智能机器人集群服务，为与会展客商营造虚实结合的元宇宙观展互动体验。进一步强化科技赋能，为参展参会人员提供精准化、便利化的无感式智慧防疫支撑。强化移动端导引服务功能，实现馆内定位导航及资讯随扫随取。设计开发进博会五周年纪念文创、进宝职业系列盲盒、进博会艺术衍生品等文创产品，展现进博文化艺术魅力风采。坚持"绿色、环保、可持续"办展方向，推进"碳中和"项目，引入碳普惠机制，打造"零碳进博"。

图4-3　第五届进博会掠影（二）

第二节　配套保障

按照习近平总书记"越办越好"的总要求，根据市委、市政府领导的指示精神，作为第五届进博会服务保障工作第十四专项工作组的牵头部门，商务区管委会按计划稳步推进各项工作，多次召开进博会城市服务保障工作推进会，加强和城保其他专项工作组的沟通联系，全面高效完成了第五届进博会各项服务保障工作任务，充分展现了商务区的活力与张力。

牵头拟订方案，全面督促落实。在征询各成员单位意见后，商务区管委会下发了《第五届进博虹桥国际中央商务区综合服务保障组工作方案》和《任务清单》。7月25日，向各成员单位下发了"工作提示"，进一步明确工作要求。商务区管委会各处室形成工作合力，协调四区两集团进一步细化具体工作任务，把枢纽应急办联席会议、城市管理精细化工作对接机制、虹桥区域城管执法联勤联动等平台作为进博保障工作的重要抓手，深入推进各项任务落到实处。针对《任务清单》中所涵盖的6个大类、23

图4-4　进博会配套保障专题会议

个具体项目，每周汇总任务进度，每两周召开联络员会议协调进展情况，不定期会同相关责任单位开展现场督导检查。市委领导多次召开专题会议，倒排任务时间表，全力抓统筹、抓协同、抓落实。

做好承上启下，建立沟通联系。管委会与市进博城保办保持密接沟通，定期上报工作进展、提供宣传素材。先后走访了长宁、闵行、青浦、嘉定四区进博城保办，以及闵行绿容局、建管委，青浦区精细办，长宁区建委等行业主管部门，详细了解各区工作开展情况，并与市水务局、市绿容局、市城管执法局等部门，就具体问题进行深入沟通对接，充分利用管委会统筹协调平台的功能机制，确保信息畅通、责任明确、协作高效。此外，商务区管委会领导多次带队实地查看张正浦、蟠臻路、蟠东路以及崧泽高架辅道、虹桥品汇二期、景观灯光提升工程等建设现场，实地查看配套工程建设进展情况，第一时间掌握一手资料。

提升市容环境，加强巡查力度。督促四区六街镇聚焦"彩化""靓化""净化""序化""优化"等方面，着重抓好商务区的清洁道路、水系、城市家具，户外广告和招牌整治、提升景观照明灯光等10项具体工作。继续发挥第三方机构巡查作用，制定巡查方案，对全域151平方千米的市容环境进行一次"大体检"，共发现各类问题987件，包括4个区、6个街镇的市容整治、道路、水系、绿化等问题。及时发现和反馈检查中发现的问题，推进问题的整改，整改完成率达99.1%。对于进博场馆核心区域、重点接待宾馆、重要迎宾通道等市容环境保障节点，分类制定方案落实"检查""巡查""督查""自查"，做到"每周必检、每点必到、每次必评"，推动各区及机场、地产等单位的进博市容环境保障工作。管委会全面深化城管执法"4+2"联动工作机制，在市城管执法局的支持下，多次走访各区城管执法部门并召开联勤联动工作会议，加强对区区交界、市区交界、城乡交界等薄弱区域市容环境的联合整治，强化地铁出入口内外和周边的环境综合治理，规范非机动车规范管理，消除环境短板，发挥联合执法的效能。

提升交通能级，整合停车资源。为了全面提升进博会期间的交通运能，管委会积极沟通协调，多个交通项目落地实施。71路中运量公交延伸工程、虹桥综合交通枢纽西交广场综合提升工程已经陆续开工，商务区骨干公交环线121路改线已实质性推进，涉及商务区的轨道交通13号线西延伸、机场联络线、嘉闵线等项目建设正如火如荼推进中，日后将大大提升往来商务区的便利性。会同闵行区，协调落实P20停车场临时启用，深挖商业综合体停车位潜力，做好进博会场馆周边停车场配建和共享，确保进博会期间工作日4 800个、周末6 000个社会停车位保障。充分发挥党组织的凝聚力和团员青年的活力，组织开展"虹桥交通驿站"志愿者服务，发动地产虹桥等单位共同参与，共计50余名交通志愿者，在虹桥天地北广场等重要点位为参展、观展人员提供引导、咨询等志愿服务。

深化应急管理，组织综合演练。全面对照进博服务保障工作的要求，走访高铁站、机场、地铁、虹桥枢纽公司，听取应急疏散和处置大客流两个专项预案的修改意见，并根据最新变化情况着手对专项预案进行更新修订。针对枢纽本体，开展安全风险评估课题研究，形成了完整的课题报告和枢纽运行风险隐患及管理问题清单。管委会结合进博保障要求和商务区工作实际，开展进博值班值守，配备相应保障资源和应对力量。管委会牵头会同铁路上海站、虹桥枢纽公司等运营单位，围绕常态化疫情防控下的密接人员转运和大客流滞留旅客临时安置两个科目举行年度枢纽综合应急演练，同时参与了首场进博综合演练，向市领导汇报了演练成果。还指导参与了闵行区（商务区核心区）商业综合体地下空间应急演练，进一步完善应急联动机制。

第三节　进博会溢出效应

　　商务区是进博会的常年举办地。商务区以进博会为契机，以建设联动长三角、服务全国、辐射亚太的进出口商品集散地为切入点，持续打造开放型经济体系，在内外贸一体化循环、产业双向投资循环、贸易合作网络形成、数字贸易枢纽建设、区域一体化链接等领域，发挥越来越重要的促进作用，会商旅文体溢出效应持续放大，长三角辐射带动效应显现，正成为国内国际双循环相互促进的重要链接点。

　　以功能平台为支撑，做强亚太进口商品集散地主功能。一是加快"6+365天"常年展示交易服务平台建设。完善虹桥进口商品展示交易中心保税货物展示、价格形成、信息发布等功能。2022年度，虹桥品汇A栋全面投入，累计吸引来自90多个国家和地区的5 700个品牌、6万多种商品入驻、销售，加速打造联动长三角、服务全国、辐射亚太的进口商品集散地。平台累计在杭州、合肥、常州、嘉兴、黄山、南京、苏州、嘉善示范区、绍兴和徐州等17个城市设立分中心，持续带动区域贸易。与上海市外办共建上海国际友城港，组织59个国家和地区的92个友好城市，进行常年的动态的主题展示、商品展销、商贸对接、文化交流等。推动东方国际贸易总部迁入平台。绿地全球商品贸易港以"引客商、促交易、优服务、强体验"为出发点和落脚点，加快汇聚国际化资源、形成市场化模式、打通专业化渠道，以更高站位、更高质量、更高能级、更高标准服务国家战略。已吸引来自76个国家和地区的180家企业和组织入驻，设立国家馆61个，引进进口商品9万余件，涵盖食品酒饮、数码家电、美妆护理、服饰箱包、家具家居等20余个大类，其中进博会同款商品超过2万款。扩大保税展示交易和全球闪电购规模，持续探索跨境电商新模式。同时，发挥平台在国际贸易、零售连锁、保税物流等领域的产业优势，上线具备信息发布、采购交易、清关物流、供应链金融、渠道管理、大数据采集等功能的国际贸易B2B综合服务平台，全力打通展品变商品的"超短链路"，成功促成50余个大类近5 000款进博会同款商品进入国内22个省市的主要流通市场。二是培育一批进口专业贸易平台。打造珠宝玉石、化妆品、康养医美、服装纺织、食品酒类、咖啡等专业贸易平台，集散全球优质日用消费品，满足消费升级和供给提质。鼓励采购商联盟加大对各国特色化、差异化优质商品的引进力度，扩大进口商品贸易规模。其中，虹桥品汇国际咖啡港已吸引30多家知名咖啡企业入驻，注册企业20多家；虹桥国际酒窖于11月5日开业，引进罗斯柴尔德等精品酒庄，人头马、奔富等知名品牌；引入专业进口商和渠道运营商进驻，注册企业10多家，预计实现贸易额10多亿元。三是进一步提升虹桥保税物流中心（B型）功能。虹桥保税物流中心连续第四年为宝玉石参展提供保税展示交易支持，一线进出口总量规模逐年呈快速增长态势，截至2022年底，全年一线进出口总额达到13.71亿元。据测算，2022年商务区保税物流中心单位面积一线进口额，在全国84家中排名第八。同时，进一步扩大保税展示功能和规模，"保转展""展转保""展转跨"等创新政策落地，通过保税展示展销或跨境电商模式成功实现"展品变商品"，进博会期间19项创新政策形成常态化安排，做强展会溢出联动。四是围绕离岸贸易和转口贸易形成新增长极。建立进博会展商贸易商洽机制，创建进博会离岸转口贸易订单中心。加快区块链技术在离岸转口贸易业务中的监测应用，支持银行与仓库、货代、船代等物流企业联网，实现数据共享、风险管控。

以数字贸易做赋能，形成进博会溢出效应转化新模式。一是做强在线新经济服务进博会的功能。鼓励新零售、网红直播带货、社交电商、社群电商等新型智慧营销与

图4-5　虹桥品汇国际咖啡港

跨境电商融合发展，建设直播基地集群和产业平台。虹桥品汇引进进宝汇直播跨境电商基地，拥有59间直播间，聚焦"直播+进博""直播+保税""直播+产业"，提供KOL和KCL主播、视频制作、内容创作、平台分发、直播培训等服务，打造以进口为主题的在线新经济平台，获评上海市首批直播电商基地，持续拓宽进博商品国内线上销售渠道。二是做强跨境电商业态服务进博会的能级。打造集品牌展示、产品交易、国际营销、配套服务等多功能为一体的全球数字贸易服务平台。集聚一批跨境电商平台、跨境金融、国际物流、综合配套龙头企业，培育一批中小型跨境电商企业。

以贸易总部促整合，营造国际贸易创新发展的新生态。一是聚焦进博会参展主体，加快吸引培育高能级贸易主体。支持引进进博展商或其代理商投资设立贸易总部。出台《关于支持虹桥国际中央商务区贸易型总部发展的若干措施》《虹桥国际中央商务区关于支持内资总部企业发展的政策意见》等总部政策，吸引跨国公司地区总部、民营企业总部、央企第二总部、产业贸易总部、本土跨国公司总部等各类进口贸易头部企业机构，打造高能级贸易主体首选地。二是搭建服务总部经济发展的专业化支撑体系。引导鼓励贸易型总部发展，提升进口贸易与总部经济能级，围绕进博会以及国际贸易链，建设"上控资源、下控渠道"的贸易型总部集群，加快建设外资企业总部园、上

图4-6　进博会虹桥品汇直播间

市公司总部园、浙商总部园、苏商总部园等总部经济园区。三是集聚国际贸易促进功能机构。支持虹桥海外贸易中心提升能级，进一步加大具有国际影响力的国际经贸组织、境外贸易促进机构、国际贸易商协会等组织的集聚力度。

以制度创新为亮点，形成国际化营商环境的新举措。一是全面提升进口贸易开放水平。主动对接RCEP等国际自贸协定，设立RCEP企业服务咨询站（虹桥），落实上海市服务业扩大开放综合试点总体方案，加大数字贸易、金融服务、商品会展等领域开放试点，将进口博览会期间的展品税收支持、通关监管、资金结算、投资便利、人员出入境等创新政策依法上升为常态化制度安排，打造进口领域全方位开放的前沿窗口。二是提高监管便利化水平。探索开展海关特殊监管区域外重点企业特殊监管创新试点。推进进口商品预先检验和预先归类服务。建立基于大数据风险评估的进出口商品差异化检验与监管机制。在一定范围内放宽进口商品准入门槛，为快运货物、易腐货物提供6小时通关便利。在保税展示交易中开展多元化保证金、银行保函、企业保函及企业资信担保等担保机制。探索货物的临时准入及无商业价值样品的免税入境政策。三是强化金融服务保障。探索推动区域认证企业开立FT账户，鼓励商务区符合条件的企业开展资本项目收入支付便利化试点，创新外汇结算，推动符合条件的进口贸易企业搭建本外币一体化资金池，探索建立"政银保"三方合作机制支持企业发展，加强融资和信贷支持。

第四节　虹桥HUB大会

　　2022年11月6日上午，由上海市人民政府、国家发展和改革委员会和商务部共同主办的第五届虹桥国际经济论坛"虹桥国际开放枢纽建设论坛暨2022年虹桥HUB大会"在国家会展中心（上海）4.2馆圆厅隆重召开。党的二十大报告指出，中国开放的大门只会越开越大。习近平总书记在第五届进博会开幕式视频讲话中指出，开放是人类文明进步的重要动力，是世界繁荣发展的必由之路。第五届虹桥HUB大会以"虹图大展·桥连世界——开放享未来"为主题，"以开放看枢纽，枢纽在虹桥"为主线，以开放中的枢纽、战略中的枢纽、发展中的枢纽为着眼点，展现高水平开放的时代机遇、高质量发展的时代要求，彰显开放主旋律，凸显枢纽新价值。

　　论坛聚焦更好服务构建新发展格局，深入实施长三角一体化发展国家战略，汇聚政商学研各界嘉宾的真知灼见，深刻诠释精彩虹桥的开放共享态度，充分挖掘虹桥国际开放枢纽核心功能，生动展现虹桥国际开放枢纽建设成果。论坛在与进博会同频共振之中，勾勒虹桥国际开放枢纽开放、建设的全景画卷。大会各项议程内容，始终贯穿"高水平"和"高质量"两大时代主题、紧密连接国内国外两个扇面、有机融合学界和业界跨界智慧，以"彩虹桥"架起双向链接快车道。全球顶尖学者与产业领袖针对新格局下的双向枢纽建设开展集中研讨，通过国际环境、区域开放、合作态势等角度，为虹桥国际开放枢纽在全球开放新格局下高质量发展建言献策，向世界发出开放共享的"虹桥声音"，不断助力区域协同创新发展。

　　论坛筹备阶段，在市商务委、市发展改革委、进口博览局等各方指导支持下，管委会把论坛筹备作为重中之重，全力协调各方资源、全力推动论坛策划筹备。一方面，注重方案策划凸显"虹桥智慧"。管委会充分调动内部研究力量和外脑智力支撑，围绕挖掘突出虹桥枢纽核心功能，尽早确认论坛总体考虑、品牌塑造、主办单位、时间地点和出席范围，利用各种资源敲定重量级嘉宾进行分享，组织撰写论坛演讲核心素材协助相关嘉宾和媒体深挖虹桥发展密码，为论坛顺利举办奠定坚实基础。另一方面，注重落地实施彰显"虹桥效率"。管委会协同组织相关处室和单位形成"综合协调、会场会务、后勤保障、接待联络、新闻宣传"等五大工作组，并多次组织专题会，按照分工协调推进、反复演练，落实"一嘉宾一团队"接待方案，确保论坛举办和嘉宾接待万无一失。

开幕环节，上海市委副书记、市长龚正，商务部党组副书记、国际贸易谈判代表兼副部长王受文，国家发展和改革委员会党组成员郭兰峰，中国银行副行长王志恒致开幕辞，上海市副市长、商务区管委会主任宗明主持开幕式。

主旨演讲和主题演讲环节，新开发银行行长马可、诺贝尔经济学奖得主托马斯·萨金特进行主旨演讲，从经济学角度强调了开放的重要性，为国际化中央商务区和国际贸易中心新平台建设献计献策。贝恩公司中国区总裁兼全球董事会成员韩微文、中国国际经济交流中心副理事长王一鸣、全国政协经济委员会副主任刘世锦、红杉中国合伙人周逵、瑞安集团主席罗康瑞等多位全球顶尖学者与产业领袖进行主题演讲，全方面、多角度分享真知灼见，推动虹桥不断探索提升服务全国统一大市场、长江经济带和长三角一体化建设能力，完善构建"四高五新"产业体系，强化打造人才流动枢纽、贸易流动枢纽、数字流动枢纽、资本流动枢纽，持续汇聚客流、物流、资金流、信息流等关键要素，全力促进长三角产业联动、企业互动、资源流动，不断开创区域协同发展新局面。

圆桌讨论环节，嘉御资本董事长兼创始合伙人卫哲、万宝盛华大中华执行董事兼首席执行官崔志辉、米其林中国区总裁兼首席执行官叶菲、百秋尚美集团董事长兼CEO刘志成、锅圈创始人兼董事长杨明超等一批有代表性的专家或企业家进行圆桌对话，深入挖掘虹桥国际开放枢纽核心功能，洞察区域协同发展趋势、解读国际协同开放机遇、挖掘区域经济内生动力。

论坛宣传阶段，管委会注重精心策划系列宣传报道。会前预热阶段，商务区核心区喷绘公益广告HUB大会主题占比超过2/3，通过主题发布、主题演绎、宣传片播放、重点采访、公共宣传阵地推广传播等，围绕主题诠释"虹桥HUB大会"品牌，体现商务区的国际化、开放度、枢纽力，引发关注与期待。会议举办期间，通过全方位、多角度、立体化的集中宣传报道着力扩大"虹桥HUB大会"传播力和影响力。会议直播传播量达到数万量级，同步扩大论坛互联网传播力。会后延伸报道期间，通过会议成果提炼、精彩集锦回放、内容深加工等后续报道持续扩大影响。《人民日报》、新华社及《光明日报》《解放日报》《第一财经》等中央与地方媒体推出系列文字与视频报道，《新闻联播》《朝闻天下》等权威节目重点播出，引发上亿量级阅读与播放量。

大会嘉宾一致表示，商务区作为国际开放枢纽核心承载区拥有持续升级的潜力。

充分发挥虹桥交通枢纽门户功能，加快构建跨区域轨道交通网，完善空铁联运模式，促进资源要素流动和区域协同发展。枢纽的发展形态由交通枢纽向资源要素枢纽演进，发展模式由单一功能向多元功能融合转变，核心功能由货物集散向智能网络平台转化，辐射空间由周边区域向更大空间尺度扩展。枢纽让经济要素聚集得更紧密，使得人工、制造、研发在内的各项成本最小化，通过缩短距离提升效率，包括物流效率和购物便利性，进而可以享受规模收益增加带来的益处。商务区都具有良好的战略地位，将成为长三角建立"空间经济"新模式的强大助力，并有潜力成为世界级的智慧基础设施枢纽，为中国现代化和全球可持续发展做出贡献。

大会嘉宾一致期待，商务区未来必将取得更大的发展成绩。围绕上海"3+6"主导产业以及发展"五型经济"要求，《虹桥国际中央商务区产业发展规划》近期已编制完成并发布，提出到2025年，努力构建"四高五新"产业体系，并定期滚动完善调整；布局建设"高流量贸易经济、高端化服务经济、数字新经济、时尚新消费"四个千亿级产业生态集群，培育发展"生命新科技、汽车新势力、低碳新能源"三个500亿级产业集群。

图 4-7　虹桥国际开放枢纽建设论坛暨 2022 虹桥 HUB 大会

第五章　四大片区协同发展

第一节　闵行片区

闵行区深入贯彻落实虹桥国际开放枢纽国家战略和市委、市政府决策部署，全面推动核心区经济高质量发展和虹桥主城前湾地区高品质开发建设，实现了国际化中央商务区快速强功能、国际贸易平台快速提能级、国际化主城快速出亮点，持续推动商务区（闵行部分）加快打造成为虹桥国际开放枢纽核心功能承载区、服务长三角一体化的桥头堡。

高效率推进政策措施落地见效，加快打造创新政策策源地。放大政策落地效应，聚焦《总体方案》29项政策，闵行区积极搭建应用场景，配套相关措施，推动跨境金融、外资准入、人才管理改革等16项政策落地操作。其中，虹桥国际开放枢纽专项债、社会办医疗机构配置大型医疗设备、长三角商标受理窗口、艺术品"展转保"等多项政策在全市率先应用，众多市场主体享受政策红利。明确重点任务目标，发布《闵行区贯彻落实市委市政府部署要求推进虹桥国际中央商务区（闵行部分）建设行动方案》，明确把握重大机遇、提升核心功能、突破瓶颈制约、凝聚各方力量等21项重点任务和60个重点项目清单。同步在此基础上分解细化成三大板块97项任务，作为闵行贯彻落实国家战略的重要抓手，加快推进商务区（闵行部分）的经济发展与开发建设。

高标准建设中央商务区，加快打造总部经济首选地。充分发挥虹桥国际开放枢纽国家战略赋能优势和"大交通、大会展、大商务"功能集聚优势，围绕"五型经济"蓄势发力，主动出击加大招商力度，"清楼扫地"释放存量空间载体，多措并举、精细服务，核心区实现企业入驻数每年保持40%左右的快速增长，累计落户企业9 000余家。其中，以壳牌、罗氏诊断等为代表的外资企业490家，安踏、锅圈、红星美凯龙等具有总部功能企业222家（其中经市级认定的跨国公司地区总部17家、民营企业总部7家、贸易型总部2家、上市公司3家），初步形成外资、国资、民营企业尤其是长三角企业总部扎堆落户的良好态势。2022年，在疫情及房地产行业影响下，区域经济仍呈现出抗风险能力强、恢复态势明显的特征。商务区（闵行部分）完成税收收入68.29亿元；剔除留抵退因素后，完成税收收入76.65亿元，同比增长12%。核心区新增实际到位外资等多项指标逆势增长；百万以上税收企业达405家，合计税收38.5亿元，同比增长11.8%；新增跨国公司地区总部3家（洛泰、美迪、魏德曼）、内资总部7家、贸易型总部2家，联合地产集团等推动恒力总部项目顺利开工，零星地块土地全生命周期管理新模式探索取得成功。

高水平打造功能型平台，加快构建要素出入境集散地。在持续提升既有平台功能效益的基础上，搭建商务区企业服务中心等一批高能级专业服务新平台，形成国际贸易、高端人才、国际法律等多领域平台集聚效应。虹桥进口商品展示交易中心一期已建成40万平方米，汇集来自90多个国家和地区的7 000多个品牌、7万多款商品，其中进博会相关商品占比70%；二期A栋新展销空间正式启用，成功打通"展转保、保转销"通路；在全国设立昆山、黄山等17家分中心，已成为集保税展示、商品交易、物流仓储、通关服务于一体的常年展示交易主平台。虹桥国际商务人才港建设取得突破性进展，中国上海人力资源服务产业园区虹桥园（国家级产业园）经国家人社部批复同意，于2022年2月25日正式开园，已落地105家行业知名人力资源服务企业，集聚和服务海内外人才，打造国际人才高地。上海虹桥国际中央法务区陆续吸引27家律师事务所和1家公证机构、5家法律科技公司落地，成功签约长三角仲裁一体化联盟等机构，加快建设面向长三角、辐射全国、联通国际的法律服务"新地标"。商务区企业服务中心已于2022年2月14日正式启用，开设综合服务、专项特色服务、外籍人士服务、"虹管家"服务等特色窗口，实现35个高频事项长三角通办、400多项政务服务跨四区通办，为企业提供全方位优质服务，加快打造商务区政务服务旗舰店。

高质量发展特色产业集群，加快构筑长三角研发总部新高地。充分发挥开放枢纽国家战略政策优势和区位优势，持续加强与长三角周边区域的产业联动合作，加快生物医药、活力文娱、数字经济等重点领域产业布局。南虹桥已集聚一批行业龙头企业，成功授牌为三大市级民营企业总部集聚区之一。生物医药产业链基本成型，依托复旦国际医疗园区，快速集聚落地了信达生物、云南白药、威高等10余家生物医药研发总部（5家已开工，其中2022年新开工东软项目实现"拿地即开工"，从拿地到开工仅用

图5-1　信达生物上海全球研发中心现场图

3天），累计投资额超150亿元，初步形成了集研发、临床、服务于一体的大健康产业集群。活力文娱生态圈初具雏形，投资超50亿元的国际文创电竞中心项目正加快建设，并联动核心区皇族电竞（RNG）等龙头项目，进一步筑牢电竞产业链优势。数字经济和绿色低碳产业正加速布局，已成功引进天合光能、赛意等项目签约落地。

高起点抓好区域品质，加快打造高品质人民城市样板间。结合商务区"区域品质提升"专项行动，加快推进核心区四大绿地、中央大道、景观灯光、商业业态、职住平衡等专项方案设计，打造国际化品质风貌示范区。坚持前湾地区高标准规划和高品质开发，在三个单元控详修编正式获批基础上，邀请国际一流设计机构，聚焦前湾10平方千米重点开发区域，按照地上、地下、云端一体化建设思路，开展城市设计深化研究，形成了可落地可实施的虹桥主城前湾地区城市一体化设计深化方案，加快建设虹桥国际开放枢纽的核心功能承载区、面向国际国内的世界级"会客厅"、引领高品质生活的人民城市样板区、服务长三角和全国发展的强劲活跃增长极。方案以"无限城市，未来前湾"为愿景，通过"无限渗透、无限魅力、无限链接、无限活力、无限生活"五大设计策略，描绘出一张"城市友好、高度适宜、路网密集、建筑通透、色彩明朗、线条简洁"的城市蓝图。前湾公园方案亮点突出，公园总面积76万平方米，围绕长三角生态绿色会客厅和世界级城市滨水中央公园的总体定位，依托带状蓝绿空间形成"一湾、两湖、三区、十八景"的景观格局。公园以C型水系为主要脉络,通过融合中西方园林的设计理念和手法,再现"城水共生"的盛世美景,打造上海西翼生态新地标。11月1日,前湾公园一期已正式开工建设。

高水平推进区域开发建设,加快打造国际化产城融合示范标杆。前湾地区历经几轮开发建设,共投入300多亿元资金,腾出了10平方千米建设空间,全力承载高能级产业集群和城市功能。2022年,按照基础设施和公共服务设施先行、优先构建蓝绿空间的开发原则,同步充分发挥前湾40亿元政府专项债资金支撑作用,加快推进道路、水系、绿化、公服等各类建设项目,重点抓好华东师范大学新虹桥实验幼儿园、四大绿地、申长北路等项目开工前期准备,同步深化研究虹桥国际文化艺术中心等重大功能性项目方案,加快构建生态健康、智慧活力、多元文化共融的国际化宜居环境。

图5-2 虹桥主城前湾地区城市设计效果图

第二节　长宁片区

对接两大战略，成立东虹桥发展办公室（简称"东虹办"）。主动对接商务区"1+1+4+X"的协调工作机制，以现有实体化的临空办、临空公司为基础，进行职能整合、空间拓展，成立东虹办，与临空公司合署办公，实现实体化运作，统筹承担商务区长宁片区的日常工作。参照商务区管委会及周边三区"管委办+功能性国企"模式，充实内设部室，东虹办下设综合管理部、战略发展部、投促商务部、规划建设部等内设部室。强化与各方联动协同的工作力度，工作成效逐步显现。

细化长宁片区行动方案。积极布展"一周年"，东虹片区企业精彩展示。全面展示"数字长宁"发展历程、"3320"数字战略、临空经济园区打造上海数字经济产业引领区相关举措以及数字经济企业集聚情况。长三角三省一市相关领导莅临参观，多家主流媒体进行报道。

积极做好一周年总结，细化长宁片区贯彻落实《总体方案》行动计划，并列出2022年重点任务清单。在三省一市工作现场会后，3月4日，召开长宁推进虹桥国际开放枢纽建设一周年总结推进大会，发布长宁一周年总结评估报告，汇编形成"'大虹桥'金融政策全部落地""首例外籍人才凭永久居身份创办科技企业"等十大创新案例。《总体方案》高含金量政策，长宁共落地26项，落地率为89.7%；其中20项做到了"三具备"（即具备承接主体、操作案例和政策红利），占比69%。研究制定长宁片区行动方案、2022年重点任务清单以及"最虹桥"引领行动推进计划。对照本市2022年度重点工作，6月16日，发布长宁片区行动方案及2022年重点任务清单，梳理提出四大方面24项主要任务，以及形成82项配套重点工作，包括加快经济恢复重振、全力落实市政府新出台的支持商务区发展新一轮政策措施等任务。对照《中共长宁区委关于贯彻落实市第十二次党代表大会精神　加快建设具有世界影响力的国际精品城区的行动方案》，研究制定《"最虹桥"引领行动推进计划》，共计87项重点任务，聚焦"开放特征最鲜明""高端产业最集聚""城区功能最完备""辐射作用最突出"四大方面。启动虹桥政策升级版研究调研工作。根据协调推进机制秘书处工作安排，6月10日，制定虹桥政策升级版调研工作方案，并对区内近百家重点企业和功能性机构开展线上问卷调查和线下走访调研，研究提出制定跨境流动数据目录和白名单等10条政策建议，全部纳入市级层面文件。

全面增强"东虹桥"发展动能。加速推动"4+6+N"重点产业集聚。对标上海市重点产业布局和商务区"四高五新"发展导向，研究提出东虹桥地区着力构筑"4+6+N"产业发展体系，加速推动形成千亿级产业集群，包括开放经济、总部经济、数字经济、临空经济四大领域，航空、时尚创意、数字、专业服务、金融、大健康六大重点产业，以及绿色低碳、智能驾驶等产业新赛道，并发布重点产业目录。

依托"虹桥之源"在线新经济生态园，数字经济高地态势渐显。"虹桥之源"在线新经济生态园，位于虹桥国际开放枢纽核心区的东虹桥片区，是三个市级在线新经济生态园之一，也是上海市在线新经济在西部的重要布局。6月16日，长宁"虹桥之源"在线新经济生态园正式揭牌。生态园已建成180余幢商务楼宇，总建筑面积280万平方米，已集聚3 400余家企业（其中数字经济领域企业1 500余家），集聚了携程、科大讯飞、爱奇艺、百秋新网商、联影智慧医疗、丹纳赫等一批龙头企业。到2025年，生态园将建设成为全国领先的在线新经济创新高地和数字经济总部集聚带，成为全国经济高质量发展和数字化转型的样板间，在线新经济产业集群规模将达到3 000亿元。

开展"潮涌浦江"线上签约，打响"投资东虹"品牌。8家签约企业涵盖了航空、数字等长宁特色产业。包括"航空物流第一股"东航物流旗下全资子公司东方福达、英国特种化学品行业龙头企业禾大化学品，以及长三角生命健康产业中心等重点项目。此外，在2022上海全球投资促进大会上，长宁片区签约上海随申行智慧交通科技有限公司，投资规模达8亿元。

聚焦人才高地建设，打造东虹人才服务特色。围绕商务区人才高地建设目标，密切对接商务区管委会和出入境部门，加快推动商务区绿通服务在长宁片区落地，通过开辟投资类项目绿色通道、外国人来华工作许可及永久居留权推荐办理等海外高端人才便利化通道、设立知识产权保护区等措施，打造形成东虹桥人才服务的特色品牌。

奋力推动区域经济恢复重振。提振企业发展信心。在出台《长宁区加快经济恢复和重振政策措施》"暖才惠企36条"基础上，先后召开日资、欧洲、美资三场跨国公司地区总部及重点外资企业圆桌会议，日本贸易振兴机构、亚瑟士、博世、联合利华、康宝莱、伊顿等30家外资总部、外贸机构表达了继续投资长宁的信心。激发招商引资活力。6月16日，长宁区召开投资促进季度签约大会，签约企业投资规模共计111亿元，揭牌长宁首家公募基金泉果基金管理有限公司。同时，在疫情防控期间特事特办，

图5-3　上海虹桥海外人才一站式服务中心

协调美资杜邦系总部企业丹尼斯克完成增资9 100万美元。比如，临空园区片区围绕服务虹桥国际开放枢纽建设，不断强化与相关部门、街镇"一盘棋、一股劲、一股绳"的工作合力，全面投入商务区长宁片区建设发展。一是重招商，提升产业贡献度。对标商务区经济倍增目标，以及区投促办招商引资目标。2022年，虹桥临空经济示范区范围实现综合税收（剔除留抵退税因素）138.12亿元，同比增长30.87%；虹桥临空经济园区范围实现综合税收68.08亿元，新增落地企业462个，其中重点项目130个，上年和当年引进重点项目贡献3.73亿元。在产业项目方面，未来已来、萃锦等人工智能领域，格罗夫、置广等新能源领域，追势科技等智能驾驶领域的优质项目相继落地；在产业载体方面，园区181幢产业楼宇实现出租率79.8%、入驻企业税收落地率81.4%、单位面积产税6 212.09元/平方米。二是优服务，增强企业感受度。着力打造"一核心、双矩阵"。围绕"服务"这一核心，深入开展稳增长重点企业走访调研，建立为企纾困解难专员机制，做到知情、知难、知心，把政策送上门，把诉求带回来，把服务做到位。围绕"政策+效率"的双矩阵，用足用好市、区及商务区等各级各类惠企纾困政策，加大宣传指导力度，打好跨部门"组合拳"，让企业少走弯路，真正"应享尽享"。三是创特色，强化品牌标识度。聚焦数字经济特色产业，获市经信委授牌"虹桥之源"

在线经济生态园，作为三个市级在线新经济生态园之一，纳入上海市第三批特色产业园区。

全面加强重点项目建设。着力优化空间规划、综合交通等功能形态。研究形成东虹桥片区"规划一张图"和"交通一张网"，加快重点地区用地转型和效率提升，会同五大驻场单位，推动机场东片区"脱胎换骨"改造提升。积极推动东虹桥片区内宜家荟聚、春秋总部项目、临空12号地块、机场集团T1北地块等10余个重大工程建设。同时，加快推进外环线抬升，打造"四纵十八横"路网，更好发挥虹桥枢纽对外交通功能。

加快明基广场改造，打造生命健康产业"桥头堡"。明基商务广场，总建筑面积合计约13万平方米，由4幢楼宇组成，并转让给了东久新宜集团。东久新宜公司旨在发挥项目的区位优势，通过城市更新的方式，提升项目的科技感和创新感。同时为匹配生命科学类研发企业的要求，将进一步对硬件和设施设备进行提升，将项目转型并打造为生命科学产业高地。

推进光大安石、东虹桥中心陆续投运。光大安石虹桥中心，总体量约18万平方米，2021年12月底投入使用。商务办公方面，融甲级独栋办公、品质商业、酒店式公寓三大业态于一体，打造独树一帜的写字楼运营模式。同时融合了光大安石WELLBEING写字楼资产管理体系，定义未来办公生态圈，办公出租率已达50%。商业方面，开业率达94.6%，包含了很多长宁首店：如TOPTOY、日产、华为MSC等。东虹桥中心，总建筑面积约17万平方米，是商务区内最靠近市中心的大型商办综合体。中心拥有约3万平方米的品质商业，主力店铺有盒马X会员店、上海首个阶梯式10米深潜水池的LAS蓝时潜水。办公方面，东虹桥中心拥有约7万平方米的4栋高品质写字楼，招商蛇口华东资管公司、邮美航空、热璞科技、开勒股份等企业已入驻办公。

建设东虹桥企业服务会客厅，打造东虹服务品牌。在东虹办集中办公地精心打造东虹桥企业服务会客厅，依托长宁创投沙龙、虹桥临空企业家联合会、投资家沙龙活动等，搭平台、促合作、聚共识，并为园区企业提供绿通服务，让企业少跑腿，不断深化"四心三最"东虹服务品牌建设。

推动虹桥体育公园开发，打造体育文化新地标。虹桥体育公园位于国家级临空经济示范区，占地面积11.888万平方米，总建筑面积41 806平方米。体育公园将通过"星际体育大都会"的概念运作，将绿化和体育结合、航空航天梦与体育结合、园区与体育结合，共同打造集体能训练与航空航天知识科普的运动时尚主题空间。体育公园的建成和运营，将成为示范区重要的功能性载体，更好地服务临空经济示范区及周边社区、学校，并逐步辐射商务区的绿化长廊生态体育公园。

加快建设大虹桥生命科学创新中心，推动大健康产业集聚发展。大虹桥生命科学创新中心依托联影智慧医疗总部项目（总建设面积约17万平方米，建设智慧医疗运营总部、高端健康管理中心、国际交流培训中心、医疗大健康产业集群和高端医疗设备融资租赁中心），推进智慧医疗产业园建设；依托扬子江、IBP国际商务花园等载体，积极打造生命科学研发中心，已集聚兰卫、雅睿、赛傲等一批重点企业，着重发展生物医药高端研发及医疗检验检测等技术服务；依托IBP二期，积极打造以丹纳赫为引领的医疗总部园，已集聚丹纳赫、福迪威、泰威康等医疗领域重点企业；以明基商务广场为载体，努力打造长三角生命健康产业中心。此外，东虹桥地区还集聚了迪辅乐、贝泰妮、惠影医疗等一批行业重点企业。

全力打造"双十"项目。提升东虹桥标识度、显示度。第一个"十"是"营商环境优化十大实事"，包括5个服务平台项目，即东虹桥企业服务会客厅打造、百强企业家联合会运作、海外人才创业首站启用、知识产权保护服务集聚区投运和"富商宝"数字店小二上线；3个基础建设项目，即架空线落地市容景观提升工程实施、交通微循环改善、慢行系统便民LinkBox试运行；2个功能配套项目，即园区职工幼托机构招生和虹桥体育公园开放。第二个"十"是"载体开竣工十大项目"，根据推进计划，主要包括近两年（2022—2023）东虹桥的3个开工项目（即机场集团P-04T1南地块、机场集团J地块和东航II-K1-01地块项目）和7个竣工项目（即机场集团N1地块、机场集团T1北地块、东航II-Q7-01综管部地块、春秋航空总部办公楼、联影智慧医疗项目、宜家荟聚购物中心和长宁区351街坊3丘项目）。

构建金融产业生态圈。优化虹桥财富管理走廊布局，虹桥财富管理走廊沿拥有百年历史的虹桥路，串起新泾镇、程家桥街道、虹桥街道、新华路街道四街一镇。重点打造"一带一城两园多点"布局，围绕财富管理、投资理财、家族信托、科技金融等特色金融，构建金融产业生态圈。"一带"，以一条虹桥路为主线、串联新华路等；东西"两园"，西部为西郊国际金融园，东部以长宁金融园为核心，中山公园数字金融城整体纳入；"多点"，两园一带连接中，分布了长宁国际、融侨中心、古北国际财富中心等重点楼宇载体，以及尚诚消费金融、仲信国际融资租赁、东方国际、软银资本等金融领域企业。长宁区集聚了700余家金融服务业企业，西郊国际金融园管理资金规模超500亿，长宁金融园入驻国盛资本、中信银行上海分行等众多金融类企业。

第三节　青浦片区

青浦区在大虹桥能级跃升的新形势下，立足虹桥国际开放枢纽优势，实施产业平台集群战略，以平台经济为核心，布局推进重点项目在空间上的集聚。2022年，青浦片区全口径税收收入103.32亿元，同比增长2.6%；社会消费品零售总额101.69亿元，同比增长16.2%；实现规模以上工业总产值85.43亿元，全社会固定资产投资210.39亿元，实到外资9 986.10万美元。

一、大商贸：进博平台经济效应明显

国际会展之都重要承载区功能进一步凸显。依托国家会展中心集聚优势和展会集聚效应，西虹桥会展产业蓬勃发展，年展览面积约700万平方米，超过全市的1/3。依托"联采项目"常态化举办联合国国际采购大会、国际采购研讨会，超1 200家企业注册。2022年青浦片区实现规上服务业营收413.34亿元。

国际贸易中心重要承载区功能进一步凸显。虹桥海外贸易中心分平台、国际时尚创意展示交易中心等功能平台加速建设，绿地全球贸易港等"6+365平台"集聚欧美工商会等40家贸易机构以及76个国家和地区客商入驻，累计交易规模超500亿元，形成国际国内双循环的重要节点和虹桥国际开放枢纽建设的重要抓手。依托绿地全球商品贸易港、东浩兰生进口商品展销中心、小咖国际康养产业创新园、国际时尚创意展示交易中心等为代表的"6+365"常年展销平台，提供"永不落幕"的、集聚贸易供需各方的沟通平台，增加开放交往、创新创意、资金技术的商业机遇，为实现"展品变商品""意向变订单""展商变客商"的转化。

国际数字之都重要承载区功能进一步凸显。依托长三角数字干线，集聚以华为海思为代表的智能芯片、以美的为代表的数字家电、以北斗为代表的位置服务等数字产业，成功引入契胜、肯耐珂萨、云砺、安永安睿和以威马为代表的新能源汽车等头部企业，集聚上市公司5家、总部企业80家。

图5-4 青浦片区大商贸发展

二、大会展：展会产业发展特色凸显

产业集聚度已达到一定规模。作为片区的主导产业之一，虹桥国际会展产业园集聚上海市会展行业协会、上海市国际展览公司、英富曼等会展企业超200家，形成会展场馆方、主办方、配套服务企业全产业链。

展览面积已达到一定规模。2022年累计举办展览6个，展出面积56万平方米，接待26万人次。其中，10万平方米以上的大型展会保持在全市大展数量一半左右，国际展约占全市数量1/3左右。

"联采项目"已经达到一定规模。2022年联合国国际采购大会成功举办，联采项目已成功帮助近200家企业（其中1家境外企业）成为联合国注册供应商，在联采项目办支持下，北京未来航宇公司成功中标"联合国基金会在摩尔多瓦的ICU医疗设备紧急采购"订单。

三、大总部：总部经济集聚现象明显

青浦片区集聚了以中核建、中电投为代表的央企二总部，以美的、安踏、波司登、圆通、弘阳、格创东智为代表的民企总部，以金融行业银科控股、医疗器械行业库克医疗为代表的跨国公司总部，以独角兽威马汽车总部、华测导航、旷视科技为代表的新兴科技总部。

2022年，还引进了银科信息总部、美庐生物上海总部、契胜科技集团总部、嘉春装饰总部、灵通集团总部、惠多多企业总部等重点项目，投资总额达近60亿元，涉及地块面积近9.4万平方米。同时，西虹桥公司与挪宝能源、金双控股、中水五局、数迹智能、九天微星、太敬机器人、中核同创等一批优质新项目签约。

2022年新增各类总部型企业12家，其中，美的集团、奥克贸易、波司登、华测导航4家企业获商务区内资企业总部认定，安能聚创、德邦物流、壹米滴答、则一供应链、安能聚创、极兔速递、义达国际、中昊针织、威马新能源8家企业新认定为商务区贸易型总部，企业总部数量累计达到80家。

四、大交通：枢纽地位日益凸显

青浦片区依托虹桥综合交通枢纽，进一步提升面向长三角城市群、支撑青浦独立综合性节点城市的交通枢纽功能，开展《青东地区共建虹桥国际开放枢纽公共交通规划研究》，开展G15抬升、G50扩容及G318改扩建专项研究，完成轨道17号线配套公交枢纽的专项规划以及新城一站等停保场的专项规划，深化25号线规划线位通道，明确至华新镇和示范区联络线线位，启动前期研究工作。加强与商务区交通路网对接，在已建成轨道17号线的基础上，全力配合推进城市轨道线路建设进度，轨交2号线、13号线、17号线西延伸，3条轨交线路已于2021年6月底开工建设，上海示范区线于2022年7月开工。有序推进"缓拥堵"项目，精准施策缓解了区域内道路的拥堵情况。结合进口博览会交通组织方案推进智能交通建设，保障交通安全畅通。

图5-5　青浦片区大交通发展

五、大数字：数字产业经济效益凸显

青浦片区数字产品制造业规上企业共11家，引进太敬机器人、数迹智能、宁择数字等一批数字经济类项目；持续跟踪服务缙嘉科技、南极电商等已落户企业，成功引进一批关联企业落户；积极推进"中国科大校友会红专科创联谊会"项目加快落地，拟以中科大企业界校友为纽带，促进科创型企业集聚，打造"中科大·西虹桥数字科创谷"，将"数字科创"这一概念从学术领域延伸至产业，打造"科技创新、技术赋能、产融相持"三位一体的合作平台。

六、大健康：生物医药产业发展成效凸显

青浦片区生物医药核心产业规模以上制造业企业共5家，重点发挥微创医疗器械

龙头企业库克医疗、血管介入医疗器械领军企业惠泰医疗、医疗器械龙头品牌麦迪睿等医疗器械龙头企业的引领带动作用，充分利用小咖云数字康养创新产业园等优质产业载体，联动大型知名医疗器械会展平台，争取更多上下游优质产业资源、创新资源落地。自2018年小咖云产业园成立以来，已入驻超200家企业总部和研发中心，累计营收超3亿元；与5所知名高校共建康养人才实训基地，与百家资本搭建投融资桥梁，服务康养产业垂直领域企业300余家、国内外康养生态企业3 000余家。

七、大物流：物流枢纽规模效益凸显

枢纽计划建设总投资360亿元。虹桥数字物流装备港已获批上海市第三批特色产业园区，上海西郊国际农产品交易中心改扩建项目、上海海博西虹桥冷链物流园二期工程、鲜丰水果生鲜港项目建设持续推进。

枢纽形成的国内首个快递物流企业总部集群，总部型经济效应日益凸显，依托遍布全国296个地级以上城市的15万个服务网点，2022年，枢纽营收规模、利润稳步增长，有效支撑起地区经济的高质量发展。

第四节　嘉定片区

2022年，嘉定在虹桥国际中央商务区经济倍增计划上自我加码，提出了北虹桥商务区"三年翻番""五年双倍"行动计划（即到2023年，税收较2020年增长100%；到2025年，税收较2020年增长200%）。在区委、区政府的坚强领导下，北虹桥商务区发挥战略引擎牵引作用，优化各类机制，破解各项难题，有力推动工作开展。为更好地开展工作，年初制定了《嘉定区贯彻落实李强书记调研虹桥国际中央商务区重要讲话的行动方案》，将44项重点任务细化分解到月，全力统筹推进项目建设、产业发展、政策落实等方面工作，保障各项工作落到实处。

截至12月底，累计完成税收41.82亿元，完成年计划的72.3%；累计完成固投61亿元，完成全年任务的73.3%；累计完成重点产业总产出97.9亿元，完成年计划的118%；累计新增企业7 790户，完成年计划的77.9%；累计新引进亿元项目69个，完成年计划的138%；累计新引进总部项目17个，完成年计划的170%；"四个一批"产业项目新拿地7个，新开工5个。

截至12月底，重点政府投资项目累计完成投资1.59亿元，完成年度目标的58.7%；重大项目累计完成投资33.31亿元，完成年度目标的104.5%。

从经济指标趋势看，开局阶段起势良好，1—2月：税收15.51亿元，同比增长29.2%；固投11.66亿元，同比增长101.7%。3—5月疫情防控期间：部分项目的推进进度、投资力度受到了一定影响，经上下齐心努力、狠抓落实。6—12月：经济情况呈现企稳向好趋势。9月：单月新增1 676户，年度累积同比增长80.56%，引进亿元项目总量排名全区第一，新增总部项目数量超额完成全年目标任务。产业总产出增长较快，尤其是精准医疗产出表现突出，10月：达月度产出4.3亿元，完成率126.47%。四季度将保持决胜气势，加强工作推进力度，对照全年目标，倒排时间节点，加强督促督办，奋力冲刺年度目标。

重点区域建设不断提质增效。"一区、一城、一湾"三大标杆性项目取得新成效。北虹桥城市更新片区，首发地块动迁工作已接近尾声，完成企业和农户签约率达99%，已累计完成农户签约497户，企业签约123家，力争年内实现地块出让；政企

图5-6　嘉定片区总览图

双方已基本达成地区总图共识，已建立政企联合招商工作机制，形成了工作方案。临港嘉定科技城，首发项目"北虹之云"将于年内启动上部结构施工；"城中村"项目改造前期工作形成初步方案；二期项目已完成概念方案设计，正积极对接土地出让前期工作。虹桥新慧总部湾，一期已出让8个地块实现全面开工；凯利、澳海项目已上标准地公告，近期将完成土地出让；福隆、仪菲用地项目正全力推进土地出让工作。同时，储备了亚细亚、恺英网络、东浩兰生等13个优质企业总部项目，发展后劲持续增强。

重点项目建设全面有序推进。北虹桥商务区对标全年目标任务，以行动方案和总控计划为抓手，紧盯"四个一批"重大产业项目推进进度。蔚来国际总部项目即将完成规划调整批复工作；天瑞金和康德莱耗材项目已实现开工；华住总部项目即将实现竣工；澳康达二手车展示交易中心项目综合竣工验收即将完成；江苏国泰中心、康德莱医疗器械基地建设稳步推进。

招商引资不断蓄势突破。持续对接了毕马威中国、中国食品土畜进出口商会、土耳其食品协会等10余家平台机构，进一步加强了与虹桥资源对接，同时还建立了与地产北虹、临港嘉定科技城的联合招商机制，打出产业链招商、政策招商、资本招商组合拳。通过开展各类"云招商""云签约""云洽谈"等活动，全面推进招商引资工作再上新台阶。2022年，已签约、待签约项目16个，总投资64亿元。当前正在和美国车桥、万洋集团、迈得医疗等多个项目深入洽谈，持续打造条块结合、板块滚动、多点开花的火热招商局面。借助长三角企业家圆桌会议等活动契机，开展好"走出去"宣介工作，高举"虹桥旗"，打好"虹桥牌"，通过组建重大项目专班等方式持续跟进，做到反应迅速、协同高效，吸引优质企业落地。另外，完成了北虹桥区域空间资源载体排摸工作，制作了北虹桥新一版宣传片、宣传册、政策折页和产业资源地图，进一步丰富招商宣传工具。

城市配套建设持续完善。交通路网建设不断加强。轨交嘉闵线金园五路站、金运路站启动建设，14号线西延伸方案研究中期形成；金运路—申昆路，金园一路—申长路两条区区对接道路取得项建书批复，正在推进项目开工前期相关工作；华江路桥、纪鹤路桥、临洮路跨吴淞江桥竣工并顺利通车。

城市基础设施不断优化。实施金园四路、金园八路雨水管改造工程，缓解金宝园区汛期积水难题；加快推进沙河路、星华公路道路改造工程，完成匡巷路部分路段施工，持续打通镇域交通堵点；杨柳桥、惠平路、吴家厅等安置基地全面复工，施工建设有序推进。

公共服务品质不断提升。教育资源配置持续优化，鹤芳幼儿园、金鹤小学体育馆完成内部升级优化；杨柳中学增设小学部，与嘉定区第二中学开展合作办学；紧密型医联体建设加速推进，龙湖社区卫生服务站实现竣工交付。

第六章　打造"近悦远来"营商环境

第一节　高端城市品质

以"强统筹、补功能、聚人气、提品质"为抓手，实施区域品质提升专项行动，打造高品质公共开放空间，提升城市管理的精细化水平，探索建设国际化品质风貌示范区。

一、区域品质提升

梳理制定品质提升项目清单。结合商务区核心区规划实施评估报告，多次对接闵行区南委办、新虹街道、地产虹桥公司和相关开发业，形成了《商务区核心区品质提升项目清单（2022—2024）》。列入清单的项目共计35个，涉及绿地水系生态空间功能提升、地标性目的地和特色街区打造、交通功能完善、公共服务设施升级等方面。按项目成熟度，分为推进开工一批（21个项目近期或年内可开工）、加快储备一批（5个项目基础条件较好，2023年可开工）、研究谋划一批（9个项目启动或正在开展前期研究，成熟一个推进一个）；按资金渠道，政府投资或研究项目20个（2022、2023年可开工且已明确资金渠道的8个），企业投资或研究项目15个。对接四个片区牵头单位，梳理了2022年度四区六街镇（华漕镇、新虹街道、新泾镇、程家桥街道、徐泾镇、江桥镇）品质提升项目，共计143个，其中闵行片区56个（含7个核心区品质提升项目）、长宁片区18个、青浦片区53个、嘉定片区16个，涉及打通"最后一公里"、优化职住布局、改善市容市貌、提升公共服务能级、塑造特色街区（高品质国际社区）、打造消费新地标、政策和标准规范导则制定七个方面。

重点推进核心区中轴线（中央大道）、北横泾河综合提升项目。会同地产虹桥公司、南虹桥公司、新虹街道、瑞安公司、AECOM等设计团队，反复讨论研究三个项目的概念方案。5月25日上午，炳章、福安同志听取了中央大道概念方案，充分肯定设计理念和平面布局方案，并对推进项目尽快落地提出明确要求。7月14日、25日，志宏同志分别听取中央大道及枢纽地下大通道商业改造、北横泾滨河空间（一期）和四大绿地功能提升概念方案，对方案优化完善提出具体要求。同时，积极协调市发展改革委领导和职能部门，争取支持。7月1日、21日，市发展改革委财金处与城发处、市财政局经建处分别来商务区实地调研，并对项目建设内容划分、审批路径等事宜研究讨论。7月28日、9月29日，市发展改革委城发处又通过视频会议形式，分别就中轴线、北横泾河项目概念性方案和项建书提出意见和建议。

研究补贴政策，鼓励企业参与。研究制定《关于虹桥国际中央商务区专项发展资金支持城市品质提升的政策意见》，对企业在实施"微更新""微改造"提升城市形象、提供高品质公共服务配套、公共开放空间改造提升、城市管理品质提升和品质提升标准体系研究等方面，起到引领带动作用，体现一定公共性、示范性、先进性、创新性的品质提升项目及相关研究课题，给予专项发展资金支持。

二、优化职住商平衡

经过多次沟通，就核心区北2地块规划建设租赁住房与闵行区达成一致意见，并就该地块涉及的资金平衡事宜积极与市发展改革委、地产集团沟通协调，并会同闵行区启动了该地块的规划调整研究工作。此外，就三久机械地块、陶家角地块规划建设租赁住房事宜也与闵行区达成初步共识。并就地产虹桥提出的虹桥国际大厦非改居事宜积极与闵行区房管局进行沟通协调。

商务区租赁住房呈现类型多元的发展态势，有公租房、保障性租赁住房、市场化租赁住房、产业园区配建宿舍、存量建筑非改居等多种类型。据不完全统计，截至2022年8月底，商务区范围已建成租赁住房总面积99.59万平方米、2.13万套，在建租赁住房62.96万平方米、1.32万套。

闵行片区新虹街道已建成租赁住房19.3万平方米、4 428套，其中，保障性租赁住房7.7万平方米、1 224套，存量建筑非改居11.6万平方米、3 204套；在建租赁住房3.47万平方米、573套为存量建筑非改居。华漕镇已建成租赁住房38.06万平方米、8 978套，其中，保障性租赁住房9.5万平方米、1 839套，存量建筑非改居28.56万平方米、7 139套（面积按套均40平方米估算）；在建租赁住房13.9万平方米、2 746套，均为保障性租赁住房。

长宁片区已供应租赁住房10.64万平方米、1 939套，其中，公租房5.59万平方米、931套，市场化租赁住房5.05万平方米、1 008套。在建租赁住房28.27万平方米、6 736套，其中，保障性租赁住房27.77万平方米、6 582套，市场化租赁住房0.5万平方米、151套。另有租赁住房5.23万平方米、1 112套，已完成规划调整。

青浦片区公租房13.83万平方米、2 278套，其中，具备供应条件的租赁住房6.41万平方米、1 073套，在、待建的租赁住房7.41万平方米、1 205套。保障性租赁住房4.21万平方米、1 224套，在建商品房配建自持租赁住房9.23万平方米、1 540套，其中，已建成4.56万平方米、980套，在建4.67万平方米、560套。产业园区配建宿舍3.83万平方米、891套，均已投入使用。

嘉定片区已供应租赁住房1.58万平方米、272套，为产业园区员工宿舍。在建租赁住房1.04万平方米、139套，为商品房配建自持租赁住房。

三、绿色低碳实践区

编制并发布《2022年度虹桥国际中央商务区支持低碳实践区建设政策申报指南》，明确对绿色建筑运行、集中供能系统、海绵城市建设的专项资金补贴政策，对丽宝、国展等项目开展专项资金评审工作。

加大低碳能效平台的接入力度，接入率提升到80%以上。基于平台数据分析，试点计算了区域碳排放数据情况，对商务区核心区公共建筑运营碳排放开展评估，定量计算出2019年和2020年虹桥国际中央商务区核心区内大型公共建筑运行碳排放量分别为22.43万吨和19.49万吨。

根据市政府2022年《上海市碳达峰实施方案》相关要求，着力开展区域内建筑领域碳排放现状分析，为下一步趋势预测和目标峰值等做好基础研究，按照市住建委相关要求落实碳达峰实施方案编制和能耗公示等工作。

四、绿建和海绵示范项目

虹桥机场东片区迎宾二路N1地块办公楼项目位于上海市虹桥商务区东虹桥片区，未来将打造东片区转性地块的样板工程。项目占地面积31 619.10平方米，建筑面积49 625平方米，其中，地上建筑面积26 085平方米、地下建筑面积23 540平方米，总投资约9.60亿元。

按照绿建三星、海绵城市等建设标准，拟建成低密度、花园式航企总部办公园区。

建设单位积极落实《上海市海绵城市专项规划（2016—2035）》《虹桥主城片区海绵城市建设规划（2020—2035）》，采用下凹绿地、透水铺装、屋顶及垂直绿化、雨水调蓄池、雨水公园、植草沟、雨水回用、生态多孔纤维棉、海绵监测等多项海绵设施，并通过与绿色建筑三星措施及评价指标关联，实现海绵城市与绿色建筑两者的完美结合。

此外，N1项目海绵建设还将与绿化景观、智能化进行融合，提供科普教育展示以及三维可视化功能，未来还会考虑将海绵管理监测数据上传至城市大数据管理平台，力争建设成为上海市海绵城市建设样板工程、虹桥商务区海绵示范项目，打造"海绵+""+海绵"的3.0版海绵城市建设项目。

五、重大项目建设有序推进

2022年度总控计划内项目共计221个，总投资约1 489.44亿元。2022年度计划完成的投资约297.56亿元（其中，重点政府投资项目39.68亿元、重大项目293.35亿元）。其中，虹桥综合交通枢纽西交广场综合提升工程、市域铁路"三中心"工程、71路中运量公交西延伸工程等市重大项目开工建设，虹桥进口商品展示交易中心二期项目B栋、申昆路停车场项目有序推进。

虹桥综合交通枢纽西交广场综合提升工程项目于7月8日正式开工，新建总建筑面积超8万平方米，总投资约6亿元。上海市域铁路调度、运营和技能培训基地工程项目于7月6日正式开工，占地面积约2.22万平方米，总建筑面积7.1万平方米。71路中运量公交西延伸工程于7月5日正式开工，线路全长约9.61千米，新增10组公交站台，将加强虹桥与中心城区的联动发展。虹桥进口商品展示交易中心二期项目B栋，南坑钢结构吊装4 510吨（80%），北坑完成B1板、钢结构吊装230吨（3%）、首道撑拆除85%。机场联络线申昆路停车场及虹桥商务区申昆路片区III-G03D-02地块上盖综合开发工程，一期基坑（3、5、7）土方收底全部完成，垫层浇筑完成60%，底板施工完成30%，6号坑首道撑浇筑完成100%；1号基坑累计土方开挖完成100%。

第二节　人才高地建设

　　商务区积极与市相关部门汇报沟通，出台特色鲜明的商务区人才高地建设方案，持续打造虹桥国际商务人才港专业品牌，建设区域人才合作交流和便捷办事的一流服务平台，在高层次人才引进、国际化人才引进、优秀青年人才引进相关措施做出未来规划，不断提升商务区人才服务的核心竞争力，以人才服务推进商务区营商环境的提升。2021年9月，中国上海人力资源产业园虹桥园正式获得国家人社部批复。2022年2月14日，作为虹桥国际商务人才港实体化运作的核心承载，商务区企业服务中心试运行；2月25日，中国上海人力资源产业园虹桥园正式开园。

　　推进人才平台建设。会同闵行区在商务区核心区建立虹桥国际商务人才港展示厅，人才的政务服务功能纳入商务区企业服务中心，设置综合服务窗口提供人才引进、居住证积分、留学生落户、外籍人才来华居留及工作许可等服务事项。在东虹桥片区会同长宁区依托虹桥海外人才一站式服务中心，建立虹桥国际商务人才港长宁分中心，可办理外国人、台港澳地区人员就业，出入境证件，外国专家证，海外人才居住证（即俗称的"B证"）等事项。

　　推进移民政策实践基地建设。制定《商务区推荐外籍高层次人才申请在华永久居留的认定管理办法（试行）》（简称《管理办法》），通过国家移民管理局备案，并推进操作实施。2022年8月，已完成第一家企业外籍高层次人才永久居留推荐工作。在市公安出入境管理部门支持、指导下，会同闵行区行政服务中心、公安部门、南虹桥公司，推进商务区企业服务中心内外国人服务窗口的建设，运行以来截至9月底办理业务超1 300件。开设国际学校签证办理窗口专项服务业务，解决因疫情封控导致的签证过期、国际学校签证业务积压等问题，助力辖区国际学校尽快复工复学，已有9家国际学校的201名外籍教职工及家属已办理业务。同时，按照移民融入服务有关要求，与闵行区出入境部门合作，建设"虹桥商务区移民融入服务站"，为商务区工作的外籍人士提供政策咨询，帮助企业解决外籍人才碰到的实际问题。

　　推进人才安居。推进商务区人才安居房受理配租工作。人才安居房房源情况：旭辉人才公寓总建筑面积6 136.24平方米，共有房源112套；乐贤居人才公寓总建筑面

图6-1 中国上海人力资源服务产业园区虹桥园

积84 049.84平方米，共有房源1 561套，截至2022年12月底，共受理17批次安居房申请，旭辉已出租房源112套，乐贤居已出租房源1 323套。同时，积极对接市场化租赁房房源，排摸房源和白领需求，搭建供需对接平台，服务企业白领安居。

推进人力资源产业园建设中国上海人力资源产业园虹桥园以申昆路2377号4号楼约1.7万平方米的空间作为虹桥园主楼，吸引人力资源企业，重点引入行业龙头企业、平台资源型企业，逐步形成规模化产业园。截至2022年12月，已有125家专业机构落户园区，其中包含英格玛集团、社保科技、上海外服、欢创集团、中蕴集团、信华人力集团等优质企业。

第三节　全力打造走出去"桥头堡"

结合外向型企业的实际需求，在商务区推动上海"一带一路"综合服务中心功能落地，会同市发展改革委、市商务委、市贸促会等有关部门制定专项实施方案，着力打造企业"走出去"一站式服务窗口，为本土企业"走出去"提供有力支持。

一是全面推进虹桥国际中央法务区建设。立足为长三角企业提供国际化的专业法律服务，紧扣"一体化"和"高质量"两个关键，在市司法局、商务区管委会和闵行区政府的共同推动下，基于商务区现有发展基础，着力打造面向长三角、辐射全国、联通国际的法律服务"新平台"，搭建集公共法律服务、专业法律服务、法治研究和交流等功能于一体的综合性区域。

虹桥国际中央法务区建设已写入《上海市公共法律服务办法》和司法部《全国公共法律服务体系建设规划（2021—2025）》，市司法局在《关于推进虹桥国际中央法务区建设工作情况的报告》中明确，以面向长三角、辐射全国、联通国际为目标定位，充分发挥现有的政策、区位、交通等多重叠加优势，形成服务高度集聚、业态高度完备、市场高度开放的法律服务生态圈，先期以可视化功能平台建设运营为发力点，快速吸引优质法律服务机构入驻，搭建集公共法律服务、专业法律服务、法治研究交流等功能于一体的综合性平台。截至2022年12月，法务区内共落地38家法律服务机构，2022年实现法律服务业总营收2亿元。正在洽谈的意向性入驻机构14家，其中包括2家全国优秀律师事务所的同城分所（上海段和段律师事务所、北京炜衡上海律师事务所）。

二是正式启动RCEP企业服务咨询站（虹桥站）。2022年1月1日，《区域全面经济伙伴关系》（RCEP）协定正式生效。上海与RCEP成员间经济结构互补性强，有着良好的经贸往来基础。为进一步打造开放共享的国际贸易新平台，彰显商务区在国际国内双循环格局中的枢纽作用，商务区多次举办RCEP政策解读与线上专题培训会，助力企业综合了解关税优惠规则，充分享受RCEP政策红利。并在市商务委全力支持下，推进常态化服务平台落地商务区，于7月21日正式启动RCEP企业服务咨询站（虹桥站），持续释放RCEP规则红利，全面提升商务区外贸服务水平，打造虹桥RCEP外贸服务

图6-2　RCEP企业服务咨询站（虹桥站）

"加油站"。

服务内容包括："一站式"信息服务，通过线上线下相结合方式，为企业提供关税优惠、原产地规则、货物贸易规则、海关程序与贸易便利化、自然人移动等RCEP协定相关优惠措施咨询服务。"国际化"专业服务，为企业提供RCEP国际通行规则、国外市场规则、涉外法律环境等专业服务对接。"专业化"培训服务，分行业、分领域组织各类培训活动，指导企业申请原产地证，指导企业如何有效利用RCEP降低企业贸易成本等。"一体化"风险防范，健全境外贸易风险预警机制，协助企业有效规避和妥善处理国际贸易中潜在的政经风险和法律风险，帮助企业找到最佳解决方案。

三是积极推进知识产权保护。会同市知识产权局围绕"一带一路"国家战略，在商务区建立中国（上海）知识产权保护中心虹桥国际中央商务区维权援助工作站。8月30日，商务区管委会与市知识产权局签署"一带一路"知识产权保护战略合作备忘录，就充分发挥中国（上海）知识产权保护中心虹桥国际中央商务区维权援助工作站以及国家海外知识产权纠纷应对指导中心上海分中心的服务职能，共建"一带一路"知识产权纠纷应对工作网络体系、"一带一路"知识产权纠纷应对工作响应机制、"一带一路"知识产权纠纷应对人才培养机制，共同推进"一带一路"知识产权高效协同保护

图6-3　知识产权论坛

合作协同机制,并举办上海"一带一路"知识产权保护论坛暨上海海外知识产权纠纷应对指导专家库成立仪式。12月16日,以"跨区域知识产权保护全面协调可持续发展"为主题的首届虹桥检察论坛在商务区召开。论坛上,上海市人民检察院与商务区管委会签订《上海市人民检察院、上海虹桥国际中央商务区管理委员会关于推进虹桥国际中央商务区知识产权保护机制建设战略合作备忘录(2022—2024)》。

四是全面加强长三角一体化服务。立足长三角,扎实推进APEC商旅卡、长三角商标受理、马德里商标受理、外国人就业许可等服务事项。2022年外国人来华工作许可业务共计受理260件外国人来华工作许可申请,发放186张工作许可证(含新办49件)。APEC商旅卡业务共计受理12件APEC商旅卡申请。商标业务共计受理1 824件申请,其中535件注册、1 289件后续业务。

第四节　着力建成现代化服务体系

一是搭建"政企面对面"平台。由企业服务中心组建6人政务管家团队，落实"虹管家"与园区结对工作，走访园区、企业。开展行政办事专项座谈，与南虹桥及华漕等多个园区政务办事负责人员沟通当前办理事项的难点，一网通办系统的使用问题及企业服务建议等事项。此外，2022年6月新冠疫情稳定后，通过政企交流，了解到企业因疫情封控导致的签证过期、签证业务积压等问题，随即开展专项出入境业务，并开设了外资企业、国际学校签证办理专项服务业务，按时办结相关事项。同时，应企业需求新增"新企业首次发票受理"事项。

二是政务服务事项便利化。研究梳理主要的事项、场景、流程，方案以"统一办事入口，聚合服务渠道""夯实中心定位，扩展服务范围""精准智能服务，优化营商环境"三大核心理念为总体设计思路，将业务应用汇聚于"企业服务"与"人才服务"两大服务集群。通过一个运营平台统筹基础服务、特色服务以及企业综合数据的管理，构造一个标准数据总库以存储画像标签、企业档案、政务知识、高端人才信息等数据资源。企业服务方面，以企业专属网页为载体，以"一企一档"的数据呈现为基础，围绕企业生产经营周期，开展个性化、精准化、主动化、智能化服务，全面推进政务服务标准化、规范化、便利化，包含办事枢纽、育企服务、专属政策、投资营商等功能模块。人才服务方面，依托随申办市民云（移动端），针对人才专属服务、公共服务提供相关内容，建设"虹桥人才服务"应用。同时对政策、事项、主题、资讯等内容进行持续性常态化更新。针对商务区管委会职能特殊性，及"一网通办"相关工作特点，积极探索模式突破的方法手段，在市府办公厅政务服务处的指导下，初步拟定了数个提升服务能级的试点方向及实施方案。同时与相关区行政服务中心开展研究，就"云窗口""商务区通办"等创新工作的推进达成了初步意向。

三是数字化转型。商务区数字化转型工作紧紧围绕"五型经济""四高五新"产业体系，从"大商务、大会展、大交通、大科创"四大核心功能出发，聚焦数字底座、商务引擎、数字会展、孪生交通、科创生态、营商服务、城市管理、生活空间等八大重点任务，以"激发企业活力、推进区域协同、建设数字环境"为抓手，建设"数字要素集聚、数字平台赋能、数字场景示范"的具有全球影响力的国际中央商务区。

　　构建虹桥商务区数据资源体系，探索数据要素便利流通机制与数据跨境流动机制。聚焦"五型经济""四高五新"产业体系，坚持产业数字化与数字产业化双轮驱动，做大做强数字经济，集聚、发展商务区重点数字贸易资源，建设面向国际国内双循环的全球数字贸易港。依托国家会展中心，创新打造"元宇宙"会展中心，探索未来会展产业模式。探索建立虹桥综合交通枢纽数字孪生平台，提升枢纽应急响应能力，构筑数智交通生态体系。重点培育科创生态，布局科技创新新赛道，部署创新创业、成果转移转化、载体建设等科技创新服务体系。着力提升营商服务供给能力，打造国际化营商环境，积极争取数字经济先行先试开放政策与试点示范。聚焦城市精细化管理，重点打造市政综合养护一体化等城市管理场景，加快推进商务区"一网统管"平台支撑体系建设。完善生活数字化转型基础设施布局，丰富商务区国际化、高端化人才数字生活服务。

第五节　精细化治理

一、商务区核心区

紧紧围绕虹桥国际开放枢纽建设战略，以打造国际品质风貌示范区和精细化管理示范标杆区为目标，按照"一核三全四化"思路框架，在商务区积极推进城市管理精细化工作，使商务区更有序、更安全、更干净，为第五届进博会提供有效有力保障。

一是完善机制。建立市住建委城管处、四区六街镇、地产虹桥等参加的商务区城市精细化管理联席会议机制，拟订并经会议讨论通过了《联席会议章程》，通过相互走访、经验交流等方式促进四区六街镇在精细化工作方面比学赶超。

二是争取支持。发挥商务区管委会统筹协调优势，走访和城市管理精细化工作密切相关的市住建委、绿化市容局、水务局、城管执法局等市区两级行业主管部门，争取在精细化工作政策试点、先进评定、标准制定等方面的政策支持。配合市城管执法局，建立商务区"4+2"执法联勤联动机制。

三是抓好试点。按照"一区一亮点、一镇（街）一标杆"的要求，每街镇选取一区域（路段）或一领域（专业）作为城市精细化管理试点，涌现了以徐泾镇、新虹街道为代表的"核心区一体化养护"、新泾镇为代表的"周家浜水域环境整治美化"、程家桥街道为代表的"小区生境花园"，同时在试点过程中不断总结经验。

四是配合做好"一网统管"系统建设。与相关专业部门定期例会沟通研讨，以"小切口、深开发"为原则，形成商务区城市运行一网统管"观、督、防"基本功能框架和包括城运网格管理督导评价系统。从城运处的角度，提出区域运行生命体征预警分析系统，重点工作任务督办系统，规划、标准、导则实施评价督导系统，枢纽安全应急管理系统等多个场景需求。配合完成项目建设的可行性研究报告，并报市城运中心入库。

五是稳妥推进区域广告整治。针对商务区广告整治主体多、任务重、周期长的特点，综合平衡依法行政、营商环境、社会稳定等各种因素，协同市、区绿化市容、市场监管、城管执法等部门以及街道办事处稳妥推进区域广告整治，共完成广告阵地整治44处，调整3处，在机场、高铁站、地下通道等场所形成进博会、虹桥经济论坛暨

HUB公益宣传237处。2022年共完成户外广告行政许可56份。

二、南虹桥片区

新虹街道瞄准城市治理数字化转型，牢牢抓住"实战+管用"，紧扣"线上：耳聪目明+线下：协同处置"这根主线，围绕"高效处置一件事"，持续加快系统整合、数据赋能、场景牵引、网格画像、流程再造。构建"城运中心—处置网格—自治网格—微网格"四级治理体系，向每个"网格"作为城市治理的最小作战单元里注入执法、管养、社会三大力量，深耕数据治理整合"自治通""企服通""智慧房管""水务防汛"等多个条线业务平台，实现手机端、电脑端、大屏端多屏联动，截至2022年，已开发"智能烟感""智能电梯""违停地磁"等17类"应用场景"，汇聚"城市之感"10 567个，可调度1 100余路街面以及小区视频、3处鹰眼、2个布控球以及65个单兵设备。做实做细各类管理要素"一张图"，实时显示人员分布、视频监控、地下管线分布、手持移动端等要素，平战结合建立完善应急指挥调度工作规范，依托政务微信"统一吹哨"，做到快速"联勤联动"，实现应急可视化指挥。新虹街道依托数字孪生技术，启动建设新虹城市生命体征系统。实现全生命完整映射现实城市运行状况，

图6-4　新虹街道道路和设施综合养护

并通过数据分析和反馈，实现精细化治理；新虹街道遵循"总体规划、逐步完善"的原则，在"最高标准、最好水平、最美环境"的精细化理念引领之下，初步形成"多位一体"的综合养护管理模式，为城市运行"安全、有序、高效"增添新的抓手，让城市变得更有温度。

华漕镇积极推进镇域内城中村改造，希望通过规划建设来根本性解决城市治理的难点问题，同时进一步完善虹桥主城前湾地区城市功能。2022年已启动诸翟村和杨家巷村2个城中村改造项目，其中，诸翟村城中村改造项目划定范围约12.5万平方米，建筑面积约14.1万平方米，集体居民295户（考虑10%分户），国有居民204户，非居住房屋22家；杨家巷村城中村改造项目划定范围约11.9万平方米，房屋面积约10.54万平方米，集体居民234户（考虑10%分户），国有居民56户，非居住房屋22家。华漕镇为推进城中村改造：一是聚焦疫情防控和城市治理难题，优先推进痛点改造提升。华漕镇针对外来人口流动性较大、宅基地房屋租赁导致社会治理成本高的问题，结合本

图6-5　诸翟村城中村项目改造效果图

次新冠疫情防控问题凸显、涉疫情严重的区域，先行启动诸翟村和杨家巷村2个典型"城中村"改造，通过整体规划建设的方式彻底解决这一区域外来人员高度集中、缺乏独立居住条件、没有独立卫生和厨房设施等老大难问题，有效减轻社会治理成本。二是坚持统筹规划，同步改善提升城市界面。将老北翟支路周边城市界面的提升改造纳入诸翟村城中村改造范围，结合后续的天山西路扩宽工程，有效提升华漕南大门的整体形象；最大程度保留关帝庙等现存历史文化建筑。三是主动跨前争取政策支持，实现整体资金平衡。杨家巷村城中村改造地块范围位于集中建设区外，按照上位单元规划，未来规划为生态廊道，经分析研判，拟通过捆绑南虹桥区域开发地块的方式推进实施，捆绑地块总体规划为商品住宅，以实现整体的资金平衡。

三、东虹桥片区

程家桥街道以大虹桥和数字化转型为契机，结合辖区特色，确定以高端商务人才国际社区配套服务和社区治理行动项目为立题，积极探索社区治理与社区服务的新模式，从而用好"虹桥优势"，放大"虹桥效应"，擦亮"最虹桥"金字招牌，不断优化营商环境，推动更多投资项目在长宁落地。项目将通过"服务联合、文化联谊、自治联心"的工作路径，以虹桥路为主轴线，聚焦虹桥商务大厦营商服务中心建设、虹桥路2222弄Y型弄堂综合治理、"程心"社（"程心"space）建设，深化打造纵贯街道辖区的金色财富走廊、绿色宜居社区和红色党建联盟，优化高端商务人才国际社区服务模式，推动社区服务及营商服务资源向高端商务人才国际社区倾斜，为辖区内企业、高端商务人士、居民等提供个性化服务，并通过做优社区服务、做强社区治理，进一步加强与国际社区居民的联系，发掘社区投资资源，促进高端商务人才、国际社区居民在长宁投资兴业。

新泾镇以自身的发展现状和资源优势，谋划推动"绿色新泾、精品小镇、善治社区、乐活家园"建设。把"绿色新泾"打造成为新泾印象的最佳展示，推动水脉、绿脉、文脉深度相融。"水脉"沿循"两纵六横"自然河流，通过建成市、区、镇三级整流域滨水慢行系统实现贯通；"绿脉"依托"三纵三横"主题特色街区、生境花园、口袋公园等绿色空间的营造而形成；"文脉"则贯穿水脉和绿脉之间，将非遗特色、江南文韵等要素充分融入景观布局。把"善治社区"打造成为新泾智慧的集中体现。进一步加强治理能力，把践行全过程人民民主与实现高效能治理有序衔接、有机融合起来。在落实数字化转型中更为突出人的需求，在实施精细化管理中拓展更多群众参与渠道，在运用分类治理机制中更加注重"能人效应"释放，在开展社区自治共治中凝聚更强公共精神。通过凸显以人为核心，不断创新体制机制，让人民当家作主的制度优势更为广泛地转化为社区治理的效能，使"善治"成为新泾的特长。四是把"乐活家园"打造成为新泾特质的突出彰显，形成由思想认同到情感认同，再到价值认同的归属感和自豪感，做实开门可享的高品质居住环境、触手可及的"15分钟社区美好生活圈"、随处可得的丰富便利公共资源、随时可感的平安家园安心守护。

临空园区聚焦景观、交通、载体建设，大力推动"五个园区"建设。在景观提升方面，围绕打造"要素集聚、功能叠加、有机融合"的国际顶级商务社区目标，深入推进临空地区景观提升工程，计划年内全面完工。在交通改善方面，北翟路协和路"C"型人行天桥和两条人行地道开放通行，为周边企业白领提供更安全、便捷、高效的出行环境。在载体改建方面，深入推进工贸小区城市更新前期工作，大力推动体育、音乐公园及外环生态绿道一体化经营管理。围绕"精品园区"目标，协调园区宜家、12街坊、联影等10个开竣工项目如期推进。结合长宁全国文明城区、国家卫生区复评及进博会保障等工作要求，强化对18条辖区河道的长效监管，持续加大违法建筑、无证无照违法经营活动、户外店招店牌隐患等检查整治力度，实现并巩固园区"零设

图6-6 东虹桥片区生态廊道

摊""零违章"的良好局面。同时，围绕"平安园区"目标，深入推进楼宇平安工作室、园区心理健康服务工作室等基层综治体系建设，强化园区城市运行"一网统管"，深入推进安全生产专项整治三年行动。园区获2021年度区平安单位称号。

四、西虹桥片区

抓住新冠疫情防控相对静态管理契机，加快推进实有人口、实有房屋排摸，城运平台城市数字体征不断完善。上线西虹桥一体化智慧管养平台。强化线上线下联动机制，简化问题处置流程，提升处置效率，进一步提升一体化管理的信息化、数字化水平。"一网统管"覆盖率不断提升。线上实现数据和科技赋能，线下实现高效处置，推动城市运行"一网统管"覆盖率不低于76%。开拓楼宇商业体管理。进一步推进楼宇管理平台建设工作。通过"一楼一策""一楼一卡"工作，按照"分楼施策、分布推进"的要求，以服务延伸和综合治理为抓手，聚焦楼宇入驻企业和商户的需求导向，完善楼宇管理精细化管理模式，拓展提高楼宇管理效能。推进城市生态环境进一步提升，新建天山西路北、国家会展中心绿地公园等城市公园绿地共计30万平方米，建成生态廊道40.4万平方米，陆域森林覆盖率达20.13%，生态品质明显提升。成功创建"河长制标准化街镇"，完成河道疏浚62条段共计62.279千米、河道整治31条段共计

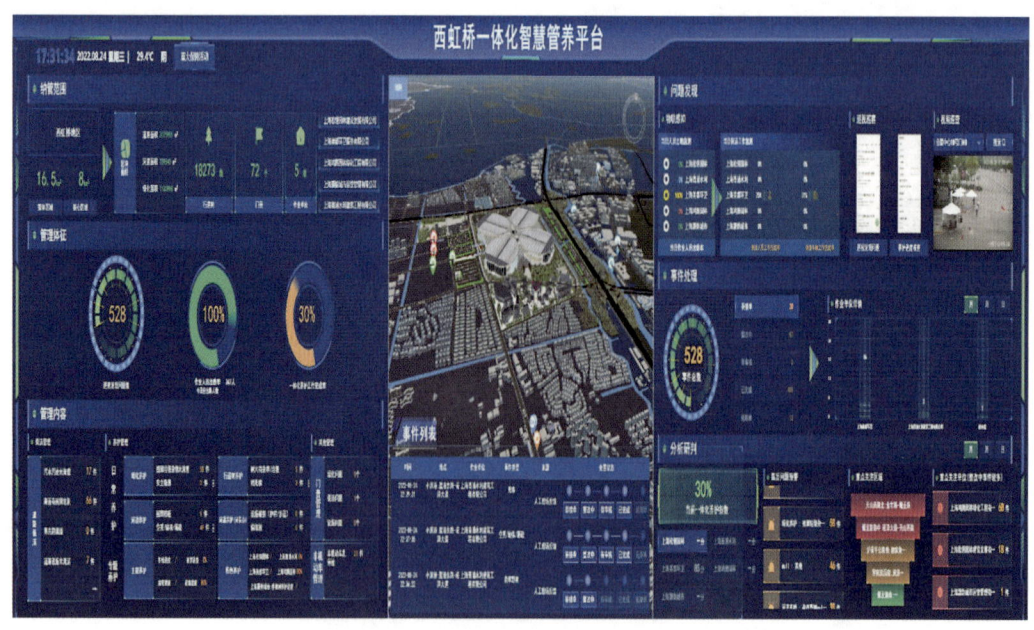

图6-7　西虹桥一体化智慧管养平台

24.888千米，全村23条段河道、1处小微水体已全面完成河道消劣工作，小涞港2018年被评为"长三角经济带最美河道"。全面完成市级重点生态廊道土地腾退任务，累计腾退面积12.9万平方米，整治违法用地10.7万平方米。

五、北虹桥片区

强力推进区域环境和安全综合整治，以雷霆手段整治一批突出的隐患矛盾问题。截至7月底，已整治违法用地9.6万平方米、违法居住155户、违法经营146起，拆除违建4万平方米，督改厂房仓库火灾隐患133处。深入开展"清洁空气"行动计划，对25家涉及喷漆、废气企业进行提标治理。推进水环境污染整治，排查梳理近130千米河道及小微水体，并制定排污口整治方案，市容环境整治力度不断提升。同时对标最高标准、最好水平，持续做好第五届进博会市容保障工作，上半年初步排摸梳理市容环境优化提升任务共计40项。加大对跨门经营、占道设摊、违规设置店牌店招等严重影响市容市貌的突出问题整治力度。

图6-8　北虹桥片区河道综合整治

附录1：上海虹桥国际中央商务区大事记

1月4日，"虹桥国际中央商务区新年企业家座谈会"举办。座谈会邀请商务区内来自新消费、新能源、新零售、电竞、造车新势力、生物医药等领域的9家知名企业的代表进行交流，听取企业意见与建议。商务区管委会党组书记、常务副主任鲍炳章，副主任孔福安出席会议并讲话，管委会相关处室负责人出席。

1月29日，商务区管委会召开2021年度总结表彰大会。商务区管委会党组书记、常务副主任鲍炳章出席会议并讲话，会议由商务区管委会副主任胡志宏主持，商务区管委会副主任付乃恂、孔福安致辞，一级巡视员陈伟利、金国军出席。鲍炳章表示，2021年是商务区发展历史上极不平凡的一年。商务区管委会全体同志紧紧围绕中央和市委、市政府决策部署，扎实推进"七个专项行动"，经济增长呈现新动能、贯彻落实《虹桥国际开放枢纽建设总体方案》取得新进展、区域品质提升打开新局面、协同合作展现新气象。2022年是机遇与挑战并存的一年，希望大家自我加压，知重负重，以时不我待、只争朝夕的精神，尽最大努力争取最好结果，切实扛起落实国家战略的政治担当。

2月8日，上海市副市长、商务区管委会主任宗明来到商务区管委会，走访慰问管委会的广大干部职工并向全体一线工作人员致以节日问候和新春祝福。宗明表示，为全面贯彻落实虹桥国际开放枢纽建设的决策部署和市委、市政府工作要求，商务区正在进行二次创业，责任重大，使命光荣，在管委会领导班子带领下，商务区管委会呈现出新气象，希望大家新的一年里再接再厉，再创辉煌，主动服务构建新发展格局，在加快虹桥国际开放枢纽建设、关注核心功能打造、形成合力聚焦发展等方面展现更大担当、实现更大作为，推进长三角高质量一体化发展，更好服务全市经济社会发展大局，以实际行动迎接党的二十大和市第十二次党代会胜利召开。

2月14日，商务区管委会与闵行区在商务区核心区完成企业服务中心旗舰店建设，在功能布局、软硬装修、环境氛围等全面优化，设立了综窗服务、专窗服务、外籍人士、虹管家服务、营商会客厅、自助办理区等功能区，实现了 35 个高频事项长三角通办、400 多项政务服务无差别咨询受理。2 月 14 日，对外试运行服务，在虹桥国际开放枢纽一周年之际，接待了国家发展改革委和长三角三省一市领导。同时，引入了外商投资企业投诉窗口、RCEP 企业服务咨询窗口，通过不断引入服务资源拓展服务功能。

2 月 17 日，商务区长宁片区举办早餐会（第一期）。商务区管委会党组书记、常务副主任鲍炳章和长宁区委书记王岚，与东方航空、中国航油、民航华东管理局、华东空管局、上海机场集团等五家单位负责人参加。早餐会上，各单位聚焦新形势、新背景下商务区长宁片区的战略定位、推进思路、机遇挑战以及虹桥机场东片区的功能定位和空间布局优化，围绕"十四五"主要项目、加强顶层设计、运用智慧交通提升商务区互联互通便利度等方面进行了深入讨论。

2 月底，在核心区与闵行区完成虹桥国际商务人才港展示厅建设。作为人才港的重要组成部分，2 月 25 日，中国上海人力资源产业园虹桥园正式开园。产业园将申昆路 2377 号 4 号楼约 1.7 万平方米的空间作为虹桥园主楼，吸引人力资源企业，重点引入行业龙头企业、平台资源型企业，逐步形成规模化产业园，累计引进企业机构 125 家，构建人才、人力资源服务的市场化平台。

3 月 1 日，虹桥国际开放枢纽建设启动建设一周年工作现场会召开。推动长三角一体化发展领导小组副组长、上海市委书记李强在会上强调，要深入学习贯彻习近平总书记关于推动长三角一体化发展的重要讲话和指示批示精神，按照中央决策部署，进一步凝聚共识、协同行动，加快推进落实《虹桥国际开放枢纽建设总体方案》，着力做强区域核心功能、推动政策制度创新、强化关键基础支撑，全力推动虹桥国际开放枢纽建设迈上新台阶，更好服务全国改革发展大局。上海市委副书记、市长龚正主持会议。推动长三角一体化发展领导小组办公室副主任、国家发展改革委副主任丛亮出席会议并讲话。上海市委常委、常务副市长吴清通报虹桥国际开放枢纽建设一周年工作情况。

4、5 月，上海市受新冠疫情影响实施社会面管控，虹桥火车站及周边区域出现滞留人员并引起社会关注。商务区管委会牵头组织会同市交通、市公安、闵行区及枢纽各单位成立工作专班、设立安置场所、优化交通动线、坚持日清日结，顺利完成滞留人员安置救助、疫情防控、客流疏散等工作，累计安置救助旅客 4 万余人，单日最高安置旅客 3 400 余人。同时，管委会抽调骨干力量，全力支持市级方舱医院建设运营和市级层面应急特需保障等工作，在打赢"上海保卫战"中体现了管委会担当作为。

6月23日，"潮涌浦江　云聚虹桥——国际贸易新趋势与企业应对暨虹桥国际中央商务区发展机遇说明会"在线举办，商务区管委会副主任孔福安向参会嘉宾做"虹桥机遇"主旨推介，吸引4 314人次观看；7月28日，商务区管委会联合中国瑞士中心，共同主办"潮涌浦江　云聚虹桥——虹桥国际中央商务区发展机遇说明会（瑞士专场）"。历时两个小时全英文的推介会，吸引了包括50家瑞士和外国公司代表在内的2 000多名嘉宾在线参会。

7月8日，潮涌浦江·虹桥综合交通枢纽西交广场综合提升工程正式开工。商务区管委会党组书记、常务副主任鲍炳章出席并宣布虹桥综合枢纽西交广场综合提升工程开工。商务区管委会党组成员、副主任孔福安主持开工活动。市住建委副主任朱剑豪、市交通委副主任王晓杰、上海地产集团副总裁徐孙庆及中建八局上海分公司、市政总院相关负责同志出席并共同推杆启动工程开工。

7月21日，商务区的RCEP企业服务咨询站正式启用，上海市商务委副主任申卫华、商务区管委会副主任孔福安共同为企业服务咨询站揭牌。

8月2日，2022上海"进口嗨购节"在虹桥品汇启动，商务区"元气虹桥·全球GO"购物节也同期开幕。上海市人大常委会副主任肖贵玉、上海市商务委员会主任顾军、闵行区区长陈华文、中国国际进口博览局副局长刘福学、上海市商务委员会副主任张国华、商务区管委会副主任孔福安、上海海关副关长邹兴伟、东方国际集团董事长童继生、东方国际集团副总裁朱继东等出席活动并共同启动2022上海"进口嗨购节"暨"元气虹桥·全球GO"购物节。

8月17日至8月19日，商务区管委会组织开展了"政府开放周"系列活动，全方位、多角度展示商务区开发建设成果，进一步提升政务公开度和市民参与度。商务区管委会的相关部门各尽其责，通过不同的主题开放活动架起了政府与市民之间沟通的"彩虹桥"。

9月1日，2022·中国上海"一带一路"知识产权保护论坛暨上海海外知识产权纠纷应对指导专家库成立仪式在商务区举行。论坛中举行了上海知识产权局与商务区管委会"一带一路"知识产权保护战略合作备忘录签署仪式，以及第一批上海海外知识产权纠纷应对指导专家名录宣布仪式。上海知识产权局副局长卫岚、商务区管委会副主任孔福安、上海市国际贸易促进委员会副会长马屹等致辞。

9月2日，商务区会同青浦、嘉定两区，在合肥举办"长三角企业家圆桌会"。现场有38家安徽企业、43名企业家参会。此外，商务区投促专班20余名招商人员同步在合肥开展了企业拜访等区域招商活动。商务区管委会常务副主任鲍炳章致辞，商务区管委会副主任孔福安围绕"虹桥机遇"全面介绍商务区功能定位和四大优势等做《打造极中极，搭建彩虹桥》的主题推介。

9月14日"潮涌浦江 投资虹桥"虹桥国际商务伙伴计划启航活动举行。市委常委、常务副市长吴清，副市长宗明，市政府副秘书长顾洪辉，市政府副秘书长华源等相关领导以及企业代表出席活动。商务区管委会党组书记、常务副主任鲍炳章做《潮涌浦江共享机遇，投资虹桥共创未来》主旨推介。鲍炳章表示商务区管委会、地产虹桥、四区政府携手国际商务伙伴，形成更具活力、更加开放的"1+1+4+X"新型区域一体化模式，创新招商引资工作机制，充分发挥政府和市场力量，各方形成合力。2022年，商务区吸引投资和开工建设项目总额近1 200亿元。其中，签约重点项目120个，意向投资额827亿元，较2021年同期增长约60%；新开工项目35个，投资额358亿。

同日，《虹桥国际中央商务区产业发展规划》（简称《产业发展规划》）发布。商务区围绕上海市"3+6"重点产业，以及商务区资源禀赋和产业基础，构建"四高五新"产业体系，编制推出《产业发展规划》。《产业发展规划》围绕"四大功能""五型经济"，强化"4311"总体目标引领，力争形成国际化服务经济与前沿创新经济集群，建成现代化国际开放枢纽核心承载区。

9月27日，商务区会同闵行、长宁、青浦、嘉定四区，在杭州举办"长三角企业家圆桌会"，现场共计有71家浙江企业参会。管委会常务副主任鲍炳章致辞，管委会副主任孔福安围绕"虹桥机遇"全面介绍商务区功能定位和四大优势等做《打造极中极，搭建彩虹桥》的主题推介。

11月1日，《上海市促进虹桥国际中央商务区发展条例》（简称《条例》）正式施行。《条例》共九章六十九条，以"强化国际定位、彰显开放优势、提升枢纽功能"为主线。围绕建设国际化中央商务区，着力构建国际贸易中心新平台，着力提高综合交通管理水平，提升服务长三角和联通国际的能力等方面，结合上海实际，对商务区发展的规划、建设、管理、服务和保障等作了明确和规范。

11月5日至11月10日，第五届中国国际进口博览会在国家会展中心举行。

11月6日，第五届虹桥国际经济论坛"虹桥国际开放枢纽建设分论坛暨2022年虹桥HUB大会"在国家会展中心（上海）召开。上海市委副书记、市长龚正，商务部党组副书记、国际贸易谈判代表兼副部长王受文，国家发展改革委党组成员郭兰峰致辞。

上海市委常委、常务副市长吴清出席，上海市副市长、虹桥国际中央商务区管委会主任宗明主持。论坛以"开放享未来"为主题，"以开放看枢纽，枢纽在虹桥"为主线，邀请国内外顶级学者和产业领袖，以开放中的枢纽、战略中的枢纽、发展中的枢纽为着眼点，展现高水平开放的时代机遇、高质量发展的时代要求，彰显开放主旋律，凸显枢纽新价值。

11月22日，商务区会同闵行、长宁二区，在南京举办"长三角企业家圆桌会"南京专场。管委会常务副主任鲍炳章致辞，管委会副主任孔福安围绕"虹桥机遇"全面介绍商务区功能定位和四大优势等做《打造极中极　搭建彩虹桥》的主题推介。

12月16日，以"跨区域知识产权保护全面协调可持续发展"为主题的首届虹桥检察论坛在虹桥国际中央商务区召开。商务区管委会党组书记、常务副主任鲍炳章，市检察院，闵行区政府相关负责人在论坛上致辞。论坛上，上海市人民检察院与商务区管委会签订《上海市人民检察院、上海虹桥国际中央商务区管理委员会关于推进虹桥国际中央商务区知识产权保护机制建设战略合作备忘录（2022—2024）》，双方将以保护知识产权促进商务贸易，助力商务区进一步发挥虹桥国际开放枢纽建设"一核两带"中的核心作用，通过充分发挥协调功能与检察职能，形成知识产权专业保护机制，为商务区创新发展提供更优质的法治营商环境。

附录2：上海市促进虹桥国际中央商务区发展条例

第一章　总则

第一条　为了促进商务区发展，推进虹桥国际开放枢纽建设，服务长三角区域一体化发展国家战略，保障更高起点的深化改革和更高层次的对外开放，根据《长江三角洲区域一体化发展规划纲要》《总体方案》以及有关法律、行政法规的相关规定，结合本市实际，制定本条例。

第二条　本市促进商务区发展的规划、建设、管理、服务和保障等活动，适用本条例。

第三条　商务区立足于构建国内国际双循环相互促进的新发展格局，推进国际中央商务区、国际贸易中心新平台和综合交通枢纽等功能建设，充分发挥全球资源配置、科技创新策源、高端产业引领、开放枢纽门户等功能，成为上海提升城市能级和核心竞争力的重要增长极、引领长三角一体化的重要动力源、落实国家战略的重要承载区，打造新时代改革开放的标志性区域。

第四条　市人民政府应当加强对商务区工作的领导，统筹协调商务区的建设与发展。

市发展改革部门负责推进商务区重大体制机制改革、综合政策制定、重大项目投资等工作，以及商务区作为虹桥国际开放枢纽"一核"与"两带"的联动发展。

市商务部门负责对商务区的会展经济和国际贸易中心新平台的协调指导，推动区域开放型经济能级提升。

市规划资源部门负责商务区的有关规划和土地管理等工作，统筹空间布局和设施共享利用。

市交通部门负责对虹桥综合交通枢纽管理的统筹指导，协调推进商务区重大交通项目建设。

市其他有关部门按照各自职责共同推进商务区的相关管理和服务。

闵行区、长宁区、青浦区、嘉定区（以下统称四区）人民政府应当按照《总体方案》、市人民政府的部署和各自职责，结合本辖区产业特色，推进商务区的相关工作。

第五条　商务区管委会作为市人民政府派出机构，统筹协调市人民政府相关部门和管理单位以及四区人民政府，履行下列职责：

（一）编制商务区发展规划，统筹推进商务区开发建设和功能提升；

（二）参与编制商务区内的国土空间规划，统筹国土空间规划的落地实施，组织编制商务区内的专项规划；

（三）编制商务区产业发展规划和产业目录，统筹指导商务区内产业布局和功能培育；

（四）统筹推进投资促进、营商环境优化、公共服务完善、人才高地建设等工作；

（五）统筹商务区开发建设计划，拟定商务区区域内土地年度储备计划，协调推进重大投资项目建设；

（六）建立管理标准和服务规范，推进城市管理精细化；

（七）建立并完善统计工作合作机制；

（八）推进政策制度创新与实施；

（九）服务保障中国国际进口博览会；

（十）统筹协调虹桥综合交通枢纽内交通设施管理以及不同交通方式的衔接、集散和转换；

（十一）统筹安排商务区专项发展资金；

（十二）指导协调四区人民政府履行商务区的相关行政管理职责，监督、检查工作落实情况；

（十三）市人民政府确定的其他事项。

第六条　商务区管委会应当牵头组织与市人民政府相关部门和管理单位以及四区人民政府沟通重要情况，协调重大问题，明确相关措施与各方责任。

商务区管委会应当加强对四区人民政府负责商务区工作的机构的指导。相关工作机构应当定期向商务区管委会报送工作推进情况。

商务区管委会可以根据市人民政府的要求建立评估机制，定期对四区人民政府依法履行相关职能和改革创新等情况进行评估。

第七条　本市根据国家授权和商务区发展需要，开展重点领域开放的先行先试，建立与国际通行规则相衔接的制度体系，吸引商务流、资金流、信息流等要素集聚，在数字贸易、金融服务、信息服务、会展服务等领域探索扩大开放措施，打造全方位开放的前沿窗口。

本市需要先行试点的重大改革举措，商务区具备条件的，在商务区优先试点。

第八条　本市建立促进商务区发展的财政保障机制，对商务区重要基础设施建设、产业发展等方面加强财政资金支持。

四区人民政府应当为商务区的建设与发展提供相应的财政资金保障。

第九条　商务区管委会建立决策咨询机制，加强与国际、国家和本市相关智库、科研机构、高校的合作，为促进商务区创新发展提供智力支撑。

第十条　根据国家发展战略，虹桥国际开放枢纽以商务区为核心，将江苏省和浙江省省际毗邻区连点成线，形成北向拓展带和南向拓展带，实现"一核""两带"的发展格局。

本市与江苏省、浙江省建立"一核""两带"规划编制会商机制，促进"一核""两带"的发展规划协同。相关规划的编制应当听取苏州市、嘉兴市人民政府及其相关部门的意见。

本市推动实现"一核""两带"在基础设施互联互通、产业协同发展、市场准入统一等方面的协同推进，形成跨区域协作新格局。

第十一条　本市加大商务区与长三角其他区域的协同联动力度，推动长三角产业联动、企业互动、资源流动，努力成为长三角畅通国内循环、促进国内国际双循环的枢纽节点。

第二章　区域规划与布局

第十二条　编制商务区相关规划，应当对标国际最高标准，实现高端商务、会展与交通功能深度融合，打造主导产业集聚辐射、全球资源要素集散、新型商业模式汇聚、基础设施联通高效、公共服务品质卓越、人文生态丰富多样的国际化中央商务区，力争成为国际开放枢纽标志性区域。

第十三条　商务区管委会应当会同四区人民政府统筹编制商务区五年发展规划。

第十四条　市规划资源部门、商务区管委会应当会同四区人民政府，依据本市国土空间规划，统筹编制商务区内的国土空间规划，加强区与区交界处的衔接。

商务区各片区控制性详细规划，依据单元规划，由市规划资源部门会同商务区管委会、相关区人民政府组织编制，并按照法定程序报请市人民政府批准。

商务区管委会应当会同市规划资源部门、相关行业主管部门和四区人民政府，组织推进生态空间、综合交通、城市风貌、地下空间等专项规划编制。

商务区内的民用机场、铁路、轨道交通等专项规划，根据相关法律、法规编制。

第十五条　商务区管委会会同市人民政府相关部门和管理单位以及四区人民政府围绕创新型产业，打造高能级总部经济、高端化服务经济、高流量贸易经济、高溢出会展经济，结合国家和本市有关产业结构调整的指导目录和相关政策，制定并公布商务区产业发展规划。

商务区管委会统一协调制定商务区产业政策和招商政策，推动商务区内各区域间的差异化协调发展。

第十六条　商务区管委会会同四区人民政府编制商务区区域内土地年度储备、土地出让、政府重点投资项目以及重大项目实施等计划，经规定程序批准后，作为市和四区相关部门推进项目实施的依据。

第十七条　商务区管委会应当对标国际先进水平，按照智慧虹桥、绿色低碳、产城融合、风貌品质等要求，制定与之相适应的建设和管理规范。

第十八条　本市围绕大交通、大商务、大会展功能，聚焦重点产业领域和核心发展指标，建立符合国际化中央商务区定位的统计指标体系。商务区管委会在市统计部门的指导下，根据实际需要，与四区加强统计工作合作。

第十九条　本市支持商务区内的保税仓库、保税物流中心发挥保税物流仓储功能，探索设立与高端商务、会展、交通功能相适应的综合保税区等海关特殊监管区域。

第三章　国际化商务服务

第二十条　本市发挥商务区在集聚总部经济、会展经济、创新经济和现代服务业等方面的作用，推动会展、商旅、金融、信息咨询等领域商务服务的国际化、专业化、品牌化发展。

第二十一条　本市支持商务区吸引、培育跨国公司地区总部、贸易型总部、中央企业和民营企业总部，实施更有吸引力的开放政策，完善国际化的专业服务，提升总部经济能级，打造高水平的总部经济集聚区。

商务区管委会应当对认定的跨国公司地区总部、贸易型总部、民营企业总部，按照相关标准给予政策支持。

第二十二条　本市鼓励各类投资者在商务区设立跨国公司地区总部和功能性机构，

支持其集聚业务、拓展功能。跨国公司地区总部依法享受资金管理、贸易物流、物品通关、数据流动、人才引进、人员出入境等便利化措施。

支持商务区内符合条件的跨国公司开展跨境资金集中运营管理，建立本外币一体化资金池。鼓励跨国公司在商务区设立全球或者区域资金管理中心。

第二十三条　本市支持高能级贸易主体在商务区设立贸易型总部，面向国内国际两个市场，提高资金运作能力，提升贸易规模，创新贸易模式。

第二十四条　本市支持中央企业在商务区设立总部或者功能性总部、研发类平台和创新联合体。

本市支持开展跨国投资、融资的国内民营企业在商务区申请设立跨国公司地区总部，拓展研发、销售、物流、结算中心等功能性机构。

商务区管委会建立民营企业总部培育名录，支持企业在商务区集聚业务、拓展功能，提升成为民营企业总部。

第二十五条　商务区管委会应当根据国家和本市部署，配合做好进口博览会招展、招商以及虹桥国际经济论坛筹办等工作，充分发挥进口博览会的国际采购、投资促进、人文交流、开放合作平台作用。

第二十六条　本市支持商务区发展会展经济，集聚具有全球影响力的会展和活动，引进国际知名会展企业总部、境内外专业组展机构、国际品牌展会及其上下游配套企业，做大会展经济规模，打造国际会展之都重要承载区。

商务区应当创新会展服务模式，提升在会展技术、专业人才、服务能力、管理体制等方面的国际竞争力。

本市支持商务区建立会展业发展协调机制，建立国际会展活动引进、申办联动机制。

第二十七条　本市推动会展和产业联动，聚焦支柱产业和主导产业，促进贸易对接、项目对接、产业对接。

商务区应当促进会展流量转化为区域消费增量、贸易增量和产业增量。

商务区可以制定促进会展经济发展的专项政策，对符合条件的会展举办单位、会展服务单位、会展项目以及会展人才给予定向扶持。

第二十八条　鼓励具有国际服务功能的会计、法律、设计、咨询等专业服务机构入驻商务区，强化专业服务业对会展、商贸、航空、金融、医疗健康等产业的支撑功能，打造现代服务业集聚区。

鼓励、吸引在中国（上海）自由贸易试验区临港新片区设立的境外知名仲裁及争议解决机构在商务区设立分支机构，就国际商事、投资等领域发生的民商事争议开展仲裁业务。

第二十九条　鼓励外国投资者在商务区设立投资性机构，对符合条件的外资投资性公司给予金融、人才、通关等方面便利。

支持优质投资性机构进驻商务区。商务区管委会应当为商务区内的投资性机构提供服务，并配合相关部门做好风险管控。

第三十条　本市推动商务区集聚研发中心。

本市支持跨国公司、国内企业、科研院所、高校等在商务区设立符合产业发展导向的研发中心。

本市引导研发中心成果转化应用，服务"两带"以及长三角其他区域建设。

第四章　国际贸易中心新平台

第三十一条　本市支持商务区拓展贸易功能，创新发展新型国际贸易，集聚高能级贸易平台和主体，促进金融与贸易深度融合，强化国际贸易产业支撑，构建国际贸易中心新平台。

第三十二条　本市支持商务区打造全球数字贸易港，积极对接电子商务新模式、新规则、新标准，推动云服务、数字内容、数字服务的行业应用，跨境电子商务等特色数字贸易。着力创建国家数字服务出口基地。

加快建设以商务区为主体的数字贸易跨境服务集聚区，促进贸易监管数字化转型、便利化发展。根据相关法律、法规的规定，探索制定低风险跨境流动数据目录，促进数据跨境安全有序流动。

第三十三条　推动进口博览会期间的展品税收支持、通关监管、资金结算、投资便利、人员出入境等政策依法转化为常态化制度安排，提升贸易自由化、便利化水平，畅通完善进口博览会商品的集散链路，形成辐射亚太的进出口商品集散地，持续发挥进口博览会综合效应。

第三十四条　本市推动在商务区建设国家级进口贸易促进创新示范区，推进贸易政策创新、服务创新、模式创新，优化功能布局，健全完善多层次保障体系，实现进口贸易要素交互融通。

第三十五条　商务区加强"一带一路"建设公共服务供给，为企业提供包括信息资讯、融资平台、专业服务、项目投资、人才服务和风险防范等方面的多方位、综合性服务。

商务区应当推动建设面向"一带一路"国家和地区的专业贸易平台和国别商品交易中心。

第三十六条　本市支持各类功能性贸易投资促进平台落户商务区，形成多层次、多功能、开放型的功能性平台体系，为促进商务区创新发展提供支撑。

本市优化提升虹桥海外贸易中心的服务功能，集聚与国际贸易促进相关的社会组织，提供高水平国际贸易服务。

本市在商务区打造进出口商品展示交易平台，发挥其保税货物展示、价格形成、信息发布、保税物流等功能。

第三十七条　本市加强新虹桥国际医学中心建设，发展医疗服务贸易，建设国家健康旅游示范基地。支持公立医院与新虹桥国际医学中心开展医疗合作，探索科学合理的收益分配使用机制。

本市支持商务区引进境内外先进医疗机构、医学科研机构和专业技术人员，探索入境监管、检验检测等方面的制度创新，加快推进创新药品和医疗器械注册上市；支持创建先进技术临床研究和转化研究中心，建设生命大健康产业集聚区。

本市加强商务区内的医疗机构建设，给予医疗服务准入、医保定点等支持，推进商业健康保险模式创新。对商务区内社会力量举办的医疗机构配置乙类大型医用设备实行告知承诺制，按照国家规定对配置甲类大型医用设备给予支持。对商务区内符合条件的医疗机构，按照国家规定自行研制、使用国内尚无同种产品上市的体外诊断试剂给予支持。鼓励商务区内的医疗机构探索跨境跨区域医疗合作，依法引进医疗技术和药品、器械。

第三十八条　商务区内符合条件的企业可以依法合规开立自由贸易账户，开展新型国际贸易，有关单位应当为其提供国际结算、贸易融资等跨境金融服务便利。

鼓励金融机构在依法合规、风险可控、商业可持续的前提下，为商务区内企业和非居民提供跨境发债、跨境投资并购等服务。支持企业开展人民币跨境贸易融资和再融资业务。

本市在商务区内对符合条件的企业开展资本项目收入支付便利化服务。符合条件的企业在办理资本项目外汇收入及其结汇所得人民币资金的境内支付时，可以凭专门凭证直接在本市辖区内符合条件的银行办理。

根据国家规定，实施货物贸易和服务贸易外汇收支便利化措施，符合条件的银行在充分了解客户和业务并开展尽职调查的基础上，对符合条件的企业实行优化单证审核等便利化措施。

第三十九条　商务区管委会应当定期编制、发布反映金融与贸易便利化程度、区域贸易活跃度、会展活动影响力等的"虹桥开放指数"报告。

商务区管委会应当建立健全"虹桥开放指数"收集、统计、分析等相关制度，发挥"虹桥开放指数"在促进商务区发展、推动虹桥国际开放枢纽建设、提升国家对外开放水平、增强国际竞争合作新优势中的作用。

第五章　综合交通枢纽

第四十条　本市全面强化虹桥综合交通枢纽核心功能，提升上海国际航空枢纽核心地位。建立虹桥国际开放枢纽连通浦东国际机场和长三角全域的轨道交通体系，完善国际航空运输协作机制，打造服务长三角、联通国际的畅通便捷综合交通门户。

第四十一条　本市深化商务区综合交通规划研究，支持商务区内区与区对接道路建设，完善商务区内道路交通体系，打造衔接轨交、扩大覆盖、联系周边的骨干公交，优化商务区与周边区域的公共交通布局。

第四十二条　优化拓展虹桥国际机场国际航运服务功能，促进优化联通国际主要航空枢纽的精品航线。

加强与周边机场协作，加大信息共享、运营管理、航班备降、应急救援等方面合作力度，推进多式联运服务发展，强化对虹桥国际开放枢纽的国际服务功能支撑。

第四十三条　本市推动虹桥国际机场获得空运整车进口口岸资质，并加强相关保障。根据国家主管部门授权，支持符合条件的企业开展保税维修和飞机融资租赁业务。

本市支持商务区发展航空服务业及其配套产业，推进航空服务业重点企业特殊监管方式创新，建设全球航空企业总部基地和高端临空服务业集聚区。

第四十四条　本市交通部门应当加强与国家相关部门以及长三角其他地区交通部门的协调沟通，强化铁路虹桥站的对外辐射和集散能力。健全与长三角主要城市之间的轨道交通网络，推进跨区域轨道交通规划协同，完善建设模式和运营机制，促进长三角跨区域轨道交通一体化。

第四十五条　本市积极推进虹桥综合交通枢纽的智能交通建设，实现全出行方式、全应用场景、全管理过程的数字化转型升级，构筑数智交通生态体系。

第四十六条　商务区管委会应当会同市交通部门组织协调虹桥综合交通枢纽内交

通设施管理。

虹桥综合交通枢纽内的交通设施运营管理单位应当根据国家和本市技术规范、规程等，对交通设施进行运行维护。

商务区内的交通基础设施由市、区两级管养，市交通部门会同商务区管委会做好协调监督工作。

第六章　产城融合

第四十七条　商务区构建布局合理、功能完备、优质高效的商务配套和生活服务体系，巩固区域绿色低碳发展基础，实现生产空间集约高效、生活空间便利完善、生态空间舒适宜人，打造产城融合示范区。

第四十八条　本市支持商务区建设高品质公共服务配套设施，依托高品质社区、高水平文化设施和城市公园，营造宜居、宜业、宜游、宜学的生活环境。

本市支持商务区通过新建、配建、改建等方式增加保障性租赁住房供应。

第四十九条　以虹桥国际开放枢纽和虹桥副中心为依托，打造国际级消费集聚区，建设一批高品质消费新地标。

鼓励企业在商务区设立中高端消费品发布展示中心，发展智慧零售、跨界零售、绿色零售等新业态，服务上海国际消费中心城市建设，打造联系亚太、面向世界、辐射国内的重要商贸流通中心。

第五十条　商务区应当提供高效、便民、优质的社会公共服务。商务区内的教育、公共卫生、社会治安、社会保障、公共法律服务等社会公共事务实行属地管理，商务区管委会负责指导、协调与监督。

本市在商务区内加快布局重大文化体育项目，引进一批有影响力的文化和体育活动，提升公共服务国际化水平。

第五十一条　商务区管委会会同市人民政府相关部门指导协调四区人民政府加强城市管理精细化工作。

商务区管委会会同市人民政府相关部门和管理单位以及四区人民政府制定商务区内道路、绿化、市容环卫、河道水系、工程设施、户外广告、招牌、景观照明等方面的建设与管理标准，建立落实相关工作机制。

商务区管委会应当加快提升城市管理智能化水平，实施综合养护一体化管理，提升城市环境品质。

第五十二条　商务区应当推动高端商务、会展、交通功能深度融合，深化"放管服"改革，健全以"双随机、一公开"监管为基本手段、以重点监管为补充、以信用监管为基础的新型监管机制，完善与创新创造相适应的包容审慎监管方式，全面推行轻微违法行为等依法不予处罚清单，加快打造市场化、法治化、国际化营商环境。

第五十三条　商务区依托政务服务"一网通办"和城市运行"一网统管"平台、国际互联网数据专用通道，加强一流数字基础设施建设，鼓励新一代通信技术推广应用，开发商务贸易、交通组织、城市运行、产业发展等方面的场景应用，以数字底座、赋能平台、数字经济等为抓手，探索具有虹桥特色的城市数字化转型建设模式，推动形成智慧交通、智慧会展、智慧商务和智慧生活功能体系，打造智慧虹桥。

第五十四条　本市按照绿色低碳的发展理念，推进商务区功能建设。

商务区管委会应当统筹指导海绵城市和绿色生态城区建设，按照绿色低碳要求指导能源系统建设和应用，建立低碳能效运行管理平台，并拓展其覆盖面。支持商务区内建筑所有权人取得绿色建筑运行标识。

第七章　服务长三角一体化发展

第五十五条　本市在商务区建设服务长三角企业和项目的平台。商务区管委会协调商务区内长三角合作事项，依托贸易展示等功能性平台，推进长三角优质品牌在商务区集聚。

第五十六条　本市支持商务区推动长三角公共服务共享，在知识产权保护、国际贸易法律服务、国际商事仲裁等领域，为长三角的各类市场主体联通国际提供便捷、可靠的服务。

市知识产权部门在商务区设立长三角企业商标受理窗口，向长三角企业提供商标注册、续展、变更、转让等服务。

注册在长三角并在商务区功能性平台备案的企业，其依法聘请或者雇佣的外籍人员，可以在本市办理外国人工作许可。

第五十七条　本市加强与长三角政务服务的合作交流，完善"跨省通办"工作机制，推进长三角电子证照互认和数据资源共享，打造在商务区的高频优质场景应用。

第五十八条　本市按照市场化方式设立服务长三角一体化发展的投资基金，主要用于虹桥国际开放枢纽的重大基础设施建设、科技创新产业平台发展、公共服务信息系统集成等投入。

第五十九条　本市在商务区建设长三角区域城市展示中心，协调长三角各城市共同打造"虹桥国际会客厅"。

第八章　服务与保障

第六十条　本市建立与商务区发展相适应的用地保障机制。

本市在市级层面对商务区内重大项目土地指标予以优先保障。按照中心城区建设标准，依据人口总量定位和产业功能定位，合理确定核心区域开发强度和容量。本市鼓励商务区内工业、仓储、研发等产业用地的多用途混合利用。

实施商住用地动态调整机制，允许按照程序将商务区内已建低效商办楼宇改造为租赁住房。

商务区探索城市地下空间竖向开发、分层赋权等土地管理改革创新，在建设用地的地上、地表、地下分别设立使用权。

第六十一条　本市设立商务区专项发展资金，由市和四区两级财政予以保障，主要用于优化规划布局和区域功能，集聚高端产业和高端人才，完善公共设施和公共服务，提升生态环境和区域品质。

第六十二条　四区取得的商务区范围内国有土地使用权出让收入，可以部分用于区域内的基础设施建设。

地方政府专项债券可以优先用于商务区内符合条件的重大项目。

支持市级新设立的政府出资产业投资基金落户商务区。

商务区内符合条件的项目可以开展不动产投资信托基金试点。商务区应当搭建项目资源对接平台，支持法律、会计、税务、资产评估等中介机构为不动产投资信托基金项目提供专业服务。鼓励四区对发行不动产投资信托基金的中介费用予以适当补贴。

在商务区内推广应收账款票据化，试行"贴现通"业务。

第六十三条　本市支持商务区在创新会展活动知识产权保护机制方面先行先试。本市为进口博览会等大型国际会展活动知识产权保护提供全过程服务保障，在区域内探索更加精准、高效、便利的会展活动知识产权快速维权处置工作模式。

商务区鼓励商业银行、担保机构、保险机构等为区域内企业创新开展知识产权证券化、知识产权质押融资、知识产权保险等知识产权金融服务；支持相关社会组织、知识产权服务机构等为区域内企业提供知识产权侵权监测、风险预警、证据收集、评估定价、纠纷调解以及维权援助等专业服务。

第六十四条　本市打造高水平的国际人才高地，建设虹桥国际商务人才港，通过中国上海人力资源服务产业园虹桥园等功能平台，吸引专业性、国际化、创新型人才集聚商务区。

在商务区加强移民政策实践基地建设，开展国际人才管理创新，相关部门应当为境外高层次人才来华执业以及交流合作提供签证、工作、居留、永久居留等便利，为外籍人才提供信息咨询、法律服务、语言文化等各类移民融入服务。

商务区管委会可以推荐在商务区内工作的外籍高层次人才、紧缺人才以及符合条件的外国投资者申请永久居留，上述人员的外籍配偶、未成年子女可以随同申请。推广外国人永久居留证件便利化应用，便于持证人在商务区居留、学习、工作。

第六十五条　符合条件的外籍高校毕业生可以凭商务区出具的工作证明，申请办理外国人来华工作许可。

本市根据国家要求，逐步放开金融、建筑、规划、设计等领域的外籍人员在商务区的从业限制，并为外籍人员在区域内居留、执业提供便利。

第六十六条　本市支持商务区引进符合国家和本市相关政策以及商务区功能定位的高等国际教育资源，开展机构、培训、师资等方面合作，培养高素质的国际化人才。

在商务区建设高质量的外籍人员子女学校，提供优质国际教育。鼓励符合条件的外籍人员子女学校面向全国招生。

第六十七条　本市创造条件，吸引各类符合商务区功能定位的高层次人才。商务区内用人单位引进的符合条件的海内外优秀人才，可以按照规定享受办理本市常住户口等人才政策。

第九章　附则

第六十八条　"一核"是商务区内涉及闵行区、长宁区、青浦区、嘉定区的相关区域，共151.4平方千米。

"两带"是以商务区为起点延伸的北向拓展带和南向拓展带。北向拓展带包括虹桥—长宁—嘉定—昆山—太仓—相城—苏州工业园区；南向拓展带包括虹桥—闵行—松江—金山—平湖—南湖—海盐—海宁。

第六十九条　本条例自2022年11月1日起施行。

附录3：上海虹桥国际中央商务区国土空间中近期规划（简版）

第一章　总则

（一）规划背景

1. 国家战略提出虹桥国际开放枢纽的战略部署

2021年2月，国务院批复《总体方案》。明确了虹桥国际开放枢纽建设的指导思想、发展目标、功能布局和主要任务，标志着虹桥国际开放枢纽成为继自贸试验区临港新片区、长三角生态绿色一体化发展示范区之后，落实国家战略的重大平台。

2.《总体方案》确立虹桥国际中央商务区的核心地位

贯彻落实《总体方案》，紧扣"一体化"和"高质量"两个关键，着力建设国际化中央商务区，着力构建国际贸易中心新平台，着力提高综合交通管理水平，着力提升服务长三角和联通国际的能力，以高水平协同开放引领长三角一体化发展。《总体方案》统筹区域发展空间，形成"一核两带"发展格局，确立了商务区的核心地位，主要承担国际化中央商务区、国际贸易中心新平台和综合交通枢纽等功能。

按照《总体方案》部署，"一核"是上海虹桥国际中央商务区，面积151平方千米，跨长宁、闵行、青浦、嘉定四区。"两带"是以商务区为起点延伸的北向拓展带和南向拓展带。北向拓展带包括虹桥—长宁—嘉定—昆山—太仓—相城—苏州工业园区，南向拓展带包括虹桥—闵行—松江—金山—平湖—南湖—海盐—海宁。

3. 新阶段虹桥国际中央商务区的战略使命

站在新的起点，从国际、国内、长三角、上海四个层级，把握商务区战略使命。

面向国际，打造联通世界的亚太流量枢纽港。彰显开放优势，着力打造全球资源要素配置中心、跨境投资贸易战略窗口。依托虹桥枢纽联通国际国内的功能，拓展虹桥机场国际航空港服务能级，完善高铁网络体系，优化轨道交通网络，建设开放联通的全球枢纽门户。充分利用交通枢纽功能带来巨大流量资源的聚合效应，充分挖掘人才、资金、商品、信息、技术等流量对区域发展的支撑带动作用，建设成为具有世界影响力的社会主义现代化国际大都市的重要功能区。

面向国内，构建全国统一大市场的关键节点。彰显改革优势，着力打造国内大循环的中心节点、国际国内双循环的彩虹桥。探索突破行政区划壁垒对一体化发展和统一大市场的制约，打响长三角"一网通办"和"跨省通办"政务服务品牌，构建跨区域协同开放和协同创新的体制机制，提升资源配置效率和竞争力，着力打造一流的国际化营商环境，为加快形成以国内大循环为主体、国内国际双循环相互促进的新发展格局，打造关键节点，提供有力支撑。

面向长三角，打造一体化高质量发展的新引擎。彰显协同优势，着力打造国际开放枢纽建设核心区、高质量一体化发展示范区。充分利用长三角一体化的战略纵深，发挥对内吸引集聚和对外辐射带动作用，带动长三角区域深度参与国际分工合作，引领带动长三角地区高质量发展，更大范围整合资源，更宽视野放大优势，更广胸怀包容合作，更高水平引领发展，建设成为名副其实的长三角经济地理中心。

立足上海，形成城市强劲活跃增长的动力源。彰显区位优势，着力打造高能级总部经济新高地、五型经济创新发展示范区。以实施多重国家战略为牵引，发挥得天独厚的区位优势和绝无仅有的交通优势，建设功能复合的国际化中央商务区。大力发展五型经济，用好用足作为上海"两翼齐飞"空间布局之西翼核心空间优势，切实承担起浦西地区中心节点与虹桥国际开放枢纽核心区之间最佳连接点的角色，带动相关区乃至周边辐射区域实现可持续的高质量发展。

（二）略

第二章 目标愿景

（一）战略定位

1. 发展目标

增强识变之智、应变之方、求变之勇，把长三角一体化发展和虹桥国际开放枢纽建设的国家战略综合优势转化为虹桥改革发展胜势，发挥空间战略上作为上海"两翼齐飞"西翼核心的地位作用，以创新型、服务型、开放型、总部型、流量型"五型经济"为特征，以面向国际、国内两个扇面的资源配置枢纽为核心功能，发挥对内吸引集聚和对外辐射带动作用，将虹桥国际中央商务区建设成为：

联通国际国内、彰显开放优势、引领带动长三角地区高质量发展的虹桥国际开放枢纽核心承载区。

高端资源集聚、功能品质卓越、创新活力迸发、人文生态丰富的国际中央商务区。

到2030年，高能级主体集聚、现代产业经济集群初显，交通枢纽功能显著增强，国际化水平显著提升，支撑虹桥国际开放枢纽核心功能基本形成，全国一流的中央商务区上一个新台阶。

到2035年，核心功能框架基本构建，产业体系雏形基本形成，区域发展格局基本塑造，活力品质城区基本显现，商务区地区生产总值力争从1 400亿元增长到6 000亿元，税收收入从346亿元增长到2 000亿元，集聚各类总部机构超过1 500家。

2. 发展愿景

（1）万商云集、活力四射的开放创新平台

建设全球城市核心功能的重要承载区。依托虹桥枢纽的联通优势、进博会的品牌优势和长三角一体化的纵深优势，融合国际化商务、贸易、会展功能，建设功能复合型国际化中央商务区和国际贸易中心新平台，更大范围整合资源，更宽视野放大优势，更广胸怀包容合作，更高水平引领发展。

建设创新引领的高端产业集聚区。聚集数字经济、生命健康、绿色低碳等重点产业，聚焦"四大功能"和"五型经济"，汇集全球最优秀的企业，展示全球最先进的技术，交易全球最优质的产品，发布全球最响亮的声音，打造效率更高、服务更优、竞争力更强、吸引力更大的高能级产业集聚区。

（2）辐射共享、内外联通的国际枢纽门户

建设开放联通的全球枢纽门户。彰显开放优势，优化拓展虹桥机场国际航运服务，强化虹桥综合交通枢纽对外服务功能，完善联通长三角全局的轨道交通网络，塑造服务长三角、联通国际的综合交通门户节点。

建设便捷高效的综合交通体系。锚固轨道交通网络，加强公共交通体系建设，完善市域线等轨道交通建设，形成连续开放道路系统格局，营造低碳集约、智能畅达的商务区交通模式。

（3）产城融合、魅力宜居的国际化城区

建设人文多元的品质社区。对标世界一流中央商务区，提供国际社区、租赁住房、人才公寓等多元住宅体系，推进人文与生活共享的社区环境，营造近悦远来、安居乐业的氛围，全面打造产城人融合发展的现代化品质社区。

建设魅力独特的活力城区。布局市级重大文化设施，做全高品质文教体卫等公共服务功能，塑造多圈层复合、多产品融合的虹桥特色社区生活圈，形成充满活力、品质宜居的国际化的新型城区。

（4）生态绿色、智慧共生的未来城市样板

建设蓝绿相融的生态之城。塑造上海大都市圈"通江达海、环城拥湖"生态网络的核心生态节点，构建全方位可持续的生态协同治理体系，营造森林环绕、蓝绿相融的生态城市。

建设低碳智慧的未来城市。倡导环保产业、绿色人居、低碳生活等发展新模式，打造低碳型城市运行方式，完善智能型现代治理体系，全面塑造舒适宜人、多元智慧的未来城市。

3. 核心功能

面向未来，商务区需要进一步巩固提升"大交通""大会展""大商务"功能，同时落实国家科技强国战略，着力打造"大科创"功能。

畅通内外循环，进一步夯实"大交通"功能。"大交通"功能是商务区的先天禀赋和立身之本，也是商务区应运而生的缘由。虹桥枢纽集散、服务功能完善，内部交通联结通畅，流量和要素聚合，以虹桥为核心的长三角主要城市群与国内国际交流密切，未来将成为全球的重要节点。面向世界、着眼未来，要进一步拉长板、补短板，加强基础交通设施建设，完善以虹桥为枢纽的上海市、长三角及全国交通骨干网络——1小时轨交达中心城区，2小时高铁达长三角中心城市，3小时航空达全国主要城市。完善以虹桥为窗口的航空枢纽港国际航线网络，5小时达亚洲主要城市。提高商务区尤其是核心区轨道交通网络密度，逐步解决内部有点无网的现状，形成由枢纽向外密度递减的交通网。进一步创新长三角区域交通合作机制，突破城市间蛙跳式交通对一体化发展的制约，通过增强交通同城化和通勤便利化，促进发展一体化，为区域高质量协同发展持续增添内生动力。

强化辐射引领，进一步强化"大会展"功能。"大会展"功能是国际贸易中心新平台建设的重要组成部分。面向世界、着眼未来，要依托国家会展中心载体优势，持续做强做优进博会品牌效应，切实发挥好其作为国家主场外交平台的战略性作用，逐步探索政府支持引导与市场驱动发展的模式。充分利用以进博会为标志的国际国内高端展览会议云集的优势，挖掘会展活动带来客商、商品、资金、技术、订单、信息等的流量价值，拓展会展产业内涵，促进会展与贸易融合发展、创新发展、协同发展，引领贸易创新，加快向离岸贸易、数字贸易、服务贸易、技术贸易拓展，使"大会展"

成为引领长三角贸易发展、促进国内国际双循环、助力全国企业抢占全球贸易制高点的战略支撑。

挖掘流量价值，进一步提升"大商务"功能。"大商务"功能是综合交通、区位优势和会展功能多重优势叠加、市场规律主导下形成的，是商务区发挥影响力、带动力和辐射力的关键。面向世界、着眼未来，商务区必须打造与定位相匹配的标志性的城区、标杆性的产业、优质化的环境、高能级的要素、高品质的配套，承担起类似横滨之于东京、拉德芳斯之于巴黎的功能和作用。产业上要持续发力、久久为功，紧紧围绕总部经济和四高五新产业，依托跨国公司总部强大的网络联结功能和全球布局能力，促进产业创新、产业升级、产业转型，做强优势产业、做大经济规模。集聚国内外高能级企业、产业、机构，在全球供应链、产业链、价值链中争取话语权。要体现经济发展高密度、高质量、高产出、高效益特点，发挥商务区对上海、对长三角的示范引领作用。

完善创新链条，进一步做实"大科创"功能。"大科创"功能在贯彻落实习近平总书记关于上海要强化"四大功能"指示精神的背景下应运而生，是商务区基于现实基础和前景展望的功能价值判断。商务区高能级科技创新主体集聚，市场主体创新氛围浓厚，科学研究和技术服务业类的企业占比是全市平均水平的3倍，市场化科创资源要素高度集聚，"应用研究—产品研发—科技服务—产业转化"链条比较完善，跨区域创新协作机制逐步形成，产业发展与科技创新耦合共生，有望形成以虹桥为核心的长三角科技创新共同体。要进一步围绕优势产业和优势产业门类，加快集聚市场化创新主体，增强市场化科技创新力量的策源能力，打开市场化主体助力科创中心建设的空间；进一步理顺协同创新机制，补全科技创新环节，打通产业创新链条，促进科技创新成果转化，打造成为上海科创中心建设的特色平台，引领长三角协同创新的驱动中心。

（二）空间格局

形成"强核辐射、多心联动，四网融合、五片协同"的空间新格局。优化交通、生态、产业、服务等资源要素配置，构建中心集聚、网络联动的空间格局，以高质量的国土空间布局和支撑体系保障中近期规划任务目标落实。

强核辐射：打造12平方千米核心功能承载区，依托国家会展中心（上海）和综合交通枢纽两大功能性设施，全面提升大交通、大商务、大会展三大功能的综合能级与协同联动发展，促进高能级要素集聚，提升东、西片区空间融合，辐射带动周边地区协同发展。

多心联动：围绕片区枢纽体系，集聚布局商务功能与高等级公共服务功能，形成南虹桥片区、北虹桥片区、东虹桥及机场片区和西虹桥片区的四大地区中心，形成辐射联动发展。

四网融合：构筑由生态走廊、绿地系统、滨水空间等蓝绿空间组成的生态空间网络，融合多模式公共交通网络、多元化开放活力网络、特色化创新协同网络，形成多网融合的空间发展架构，促进商务区空间一体化发展。

五片协同：以优势互补、错位发展、协同联动为目标，形成功能完善、各具特色、互联互通的五大功能板块，包括核心区、南虹桥片区、东虹桥片区、西虹桥片区、北虹桥片区。

第三章　空间策略

（一）推动五大片区高质量建设

虹桥国际中央商务区规划形成五个片区，即核心区、南虹桥片区、东虹桥片区、西虹桥片区和北虹桥片区。依托各片区主导功能，提出相应的空间策略，强化城乡空间资源统筹，推进全覆盖、差异化的规划举措，引导各片区总体规划、总体城市设计、专项规划等后续规划编制和实施。

1. 核心区——全球资源要素配置战略窗口

核心区面积19.5平方千米，规划可承载人口7万人。已建成建设用地占比62%，可新增开发空间共90万平方米，其中商办研发85万平方米、住宅3万平方米。

建设总部经济集聚区，建设开放联通的全球枢纽门户。充分挖掘人才、资金、商品、信息、技术等流量对区域发展的支撑作用，大力吸引跨国公司、央企国企和民营企业总部落户，提升资源配置效率和竞争力，着力打造一流的国际化营商环境。推动构建面向国际与长三角的开放贸易平台，打造创新先行的高品质商贸集聚区。

优化交通枢纽功能，增强片区对外联系，加强精细化交通管理水平。优化枢纽功能，积极推动公共交通网络建设，依托嘉闵线等市域线与轨道交通建设，推进会展中心站综合开发研究，提升交通枢纽对外辐射功能。依托中运量交通71路西延伸，进一步促进核心区与中心城区联系。结合全市轨道交通网络，研究利用原规划17号线通道建设25号线支线，轨道交通覆盖率提升至45%。充分完善核心区路网体系，全面强化与东虹桥片区、西虹桥片区、北虹桥片区联动发展。

打造人文生态丰富的活力城区，盘活存量空间，提升环境品质。探索存量商务办公楼宇的功能复合化利用，新增1万户租赁性住房供应。推进核心区中轴线四大绿地等提升工程，植入文化体育艺术类公共服务设施。

2. 南虹桥片区——高品质的世界级会客厅

南虹桥片区面积30.8平方千米，规划可承载人口18万人。已建成建设用地占比25%，可新增开发空间共750万平方米，其中商办研发335万平方米、住宅300万平方米、公共服务110万平方米。

打造面向长三角的国际化高端服务经济新门户，以国际化公共服务功能和多元高端融合的服务经济为主要特色，依托南虹桥前湾商务区、新虹桥国际医学中心、虹桥进口商品交易中心等园区功能平台，重点发展生物医药、国际商贸、国际文娱、数字经济、时尚新消费等产业。深化完善相关产业链构建，积极推动产学研一体化平台与对外贸易平台建设，打造面向长三角的国际化高端服务经济门户。

强化公共交通可达性，综合提升枢纽功能能级。建设长三角一体化示范区联络线芳乐路站，进一步突出服务长三角功能，围绕示范区芳乐路枢纽强化TOD布局。推进轨道交通13号线、25号线建设，充分利用原规划17号线通道建设25号线支线，联动虹桥核心区，至2030年，提升地区城市开发边界内轨道交通站点600米用地覆盖率至54%，局域线覆盖率至80%。

布局高等级公共服务设施，提升长三角服务能力。围绕前湾公园建设，高标准配置公共服务设施，引入国际化大学、2处市级文化设施，推进虹桥国际医学中心二期、国际新文创电竞中心、都市运动中心、规划展示馆等高等级文化设施建设。

高标准建设国际化新城区。推进杨家巷村、诸翟村城中村改造，建设南虹桥国际社区，丰富住宅品类，注入高端化、国际化服务功能。至2030年，新增60万平方米保障性租赁住房。打造吴淞江生态间隔带为活力生态空间，加强两岸联动，推动城园相融，优化提升建设用地功能与布局，提升区域环境品质。

3. 东虹桥片区——国际级临空商务新中心

东虹桥片区面积19.9平方千米，规划可承载人口20万人。已建成建设用地占比96%，可新增开发空间共50万平方米，其中商办45万平方米、住宅3万平方米。

打造强劲活跃的国家级临空经济示范区，建设虹桥国际开放枢纽的总部高地、上海数字经济转型标杆区以及全国领先的在线新经济创新高地，深化核心功能，持续蓄能临空经济、数字经济、总部经济三大高地态势，提升生命健康、金融服务、人工智能等高端服务业活力。构建特色鲜明、实力强劲的现代产业体系。强化高端产业集聚，巩固传统优势产业与特色产业发展优势，推进重点产业项目建设。

推进机场东片区脱胎换骨改造提升。深化产城融合，推动载体开发建设与产业功能同步衔接，统筹推进商业、办公、商务配套、住宅等综合开发，打造花园办公社区。推进租赁住房建设，结合15分钟社区生活圈完善社区级公共服务设施配套。

优化区域交通格局，强化交通网络联系。推进26号线和地区内中运量交通线网建设，至2030年提升轨道交通站点600米覆盖率62.8%。结合外环抬升连通地区交通网络，推进区区对接，打通断头路，完善东虹桥与中心城、核心区路网联通。

推动存量更新，编织活力绿网，打造宜居宜业的国际化花园办公社区。依托外环绿带、临空滨河休闲片区与西郊综合休闲片区等生态空间基底，植入口袋公园与多样化休闲空间，进一步推进苏州河景观廊道、外环生态绿道建设，提升虹桥体育公园、临空滑板公园、临空音乐公园、临空体育中心等公共空间与公共设施的环境品质。

4. 西虹桥片区——国际贸易和数字枢纽新门户

西虹桥片区面积38.8平方千米，规划可承载人口约29万人。已建成建设用地占比60%，可新增开发空间共700万平方米，其中商办研发460万平方米、住宅200万平方米、公共服务20万平方米。

打造上海国际会展之都核心承载区，持续放大进口博览会外溢带动效应，建设"长三角数字干线"龙头，重点布局会展经济、贸易经济、智慧健康、数字创新经济、新型供应链、时尚新消费等产业。聚焦会展商贸功能，充分利用会展经济带来的流量优势，加强高能级商贸主体的对接与引进，促进产业集群蓬勃发展，推动高端会务、广告设计等会展服务产业链延伸完善。积极培育科研创意产业发展，进一步放大北斗导航等特色产业优势，夯实科技创新源动力，打造以会展功能为引领的国际化创新集聚区。通过统筹华新镇域建设用地空间布局，落实华新片区的"虹桥数智供应链聚集区"。

建设高品质城市副中心，提升服务长三角的能力。高标准推进副中心地区项目建设，加快推进百老汇演艺综合体、国际冰上中心两处市级文体设施建设。推进长三角跨区域公共数据平台等功能性平台建设。

推进公共服务设施建设和租赁住房供给。建设4处区级文化设施、2处区级体育设施和1处区级医疗设施，全面推进社区级设施建设，结合蟠龙古镇等开放空间引导各类文创活动有序开展。多渠道筹措，至2030年，新增70万平方米保障性租赁住房。全面推进城中村改造，推进国际社区建设。

强化交通枢纽能级，分解区域交通客流。结合道路网络优化与静态交通系统建设，充分发挥会展中心枢纽对大客流交通集散功能的支撑作用，推动商务区道路交通持续改善。推进2号线西延伸、13号线西延伸、25号线建设，站点600米用地覆盖率由16%提高至29%，含局域线提高至52%。推进G15抬升建设，完善路网格局。

5. 北虹桥片区——国际创新产业集聚区

北虹桥片区面积42.6平方千米，规划可承载人口36万人。已建成建设用地占比34%，可新增开发空间共620万平方米，其中商办研发305万平方米、住宅200万平方米、公共服务30万平方米、工业100万平方米。

建设虹桥商务区"大科创"功能主要承载地。承接核心区商贸功能外溢，连接长三角制造业腹地，为嘉定对接全球经济提供创新环境及产业配套服务支持。以创新经济、总部经济为特色，培育数字新经济、生命新科技、低碳新能源、汽车新势力产业链创新融合生态集群。加强产业用地整体复合利用，提升经济密度与园区活力。以临港嘉定科技城、新慧总部湾、地产北虹城市更新片区为重点，吸引一批具有创新活力的领军企业入驻，打造国际化科创集聚区。

构建开放的公共交通网络系统，强化区域间联动。依托北虹桥商业商务集聚区的嘉闵线站点建设，北向联动嘉定新城，南向连接虹桥枢纽。结合14号线西延伸、中运量交通线建设与申长路、申昆路道路贯通，加强与嘉定新城、商务区核心区联系，充分发挥完善的公共交通网络与开放式路网格局对科创集聚区吸引人才的积极效应。

加快城区品质提升和功能转型，建设国际社区。推动产城融合，推进封浜、五四村、金虹社区等区域城中村改造，进一步优化住宅结构，多渠道筹措租赁性住宅，至2030年，新增27万平方米保障性租赁住房，定向服务本地区就业人群，提升产城融合水平，加快有条件区域建设国际社区。

协同滨江生态建设，塑造公园城市典范。与南虹桥协同推进吴淞江两岸生态绿色空间一体化建设。充分发挥滨水空间优势，引入国际科技体育中心等文体设施，以吴淞江生态功能带联动公共服务设施的共融式发展。围绕生态间隔带与外环绿带景观节点，积极布局创新创意功能空间，提升产业空间品质。

（二）政策保障

1. 完善顶层设计，探索高效开发体制机制

根据《上海市促进虹桥国际中央商务区发展条例》，进一步明确"1+1+4+X"主体的职责，强化目标、决策和执行的有机统一。商务区管委会强化顶层设计，负责区域整体规划、管理标准制定、开发建设计划、政策制度创新；地产集团推进建设实施；

闵行区、长宁区、青浦区、嘉定区人民政府发挥项目建设和项目管理的主体作用；市级相关部门支持指导、协调审批。

加强专项发展资金、土地出让收入、地方政府专项债券、政府出资产业投资基金等投入。把管委会体制的开放性优势和行政区的实体性优势发挥到最好水平，推进国家战略落实。

2. 凸显规划引领，推进下位规划高标准修编

以《中近期规划》为总体引导，基于规划确定的目标定位、规划策略、任务要求，统筹规划与建设标准，通过编制专项规划、控制性详细规划等下位规划进一步落实。

商务区管委会统筹全域规划研究，开展商务区租赁性住房专项规划、城中村改造专项规划、国际社区建设导则、吴淞江两岸生态廊道规划等规划编制。抓紧推进专项规划编制，包括沪杭铁路外环线改造利用专项规划、会展中心枢纽专项规划、G2公路入城段扩容改造及新增匝道研究、25号线支线（原17号线通道利用）专项规划、吴淞江生态间隔带专项规划等。

各区依据本规划，加快深化分片区规划研究，推进相关街镇范围内规划修编，优化土地供应结构，强化资源要素保障，并针对性启动相应专项规划编制。高标准推进控制性详细规划编制，以优化轨交站点周边用地布局，强化土地复合高效利用为原则，提高站点周边和城中村改造地块开发强度，推进重点地区控制性详细规划编制。

3. 强化资源保障，优化土地供应结构

在市级层面对商务区内重大项目土地指标予以优先保障。

按照中心城区建设标准，依据人口总量定位和产业功能定位，合理确定核心区域开发强度和容量。

土地供应重点由基础设施建设转向功能开发，提升绿地、公共服务、租赁性住房等用地比例。

商务区鼓励工业、仓储、研发等产业用地多用途混合利用。实施商住用地动态调整机制，允许按照程序将商务区内已建低效商办楼宇改造为租赁住房。

附录4：上海虹桥国际中央商务区产业发展规划（简版）

商务区是服务长三角一体化的重要枢纽节点，虹桥国际开放枢纽的核心承载区，上海都市圈西翼发展的重要增长极。为深入落实《长江三角洲区域一体化发展规划纲要》《总体方案》和全市工作部署，高质量协同推进商务区产业创新发展，编制本规划。

一、发展基础

商务区全域环绕虹桥综合交通枢纽，包含长宁、闵行、青浦、嘉定四区街镇，面积151.4平方千米。虹桥空铁一体化枢纽2小时通达长三角，3小时覆盖全国和亚太重点城市。经过十几年发展，商务区国际贸易中心新平台初成体系，新兴产业领域开拓初具方向，数字新经济发展初具规模，专业服务业集聚初显特色。在长三角一体化、进博会等国家战略叠加赋能下，商务区正成为上海与长三角经济发展的强劲活跃增长极。

二、总体要求

（一）指导思想和基本原则

以习近平新时代中国特色社会主义思想为指导，紧扣长三角"一体化"和"高质量"两个关键，结合全市"3+6"产业方向，逐步形成面向未来的中央商务区现代产业体系。坚持国际化开放发展、高能级集聚发展、新赛道创新发展、新生态融合发展、一体化联动发展五项基本原则。

（二）发展目标

到2025年，初步形成"四高五新"中央商务区产业发展体系，聚焦"高能级总部经济、高溢出会展经济、高流量贸易经济、高端化服务经济"四大核心功能产业，聚力"数字新经济、生命新科技、低碳新能源、汽车新势力、时尚新消费"五个未来产业新赛道。到2035年，全面形成具有高能级水平与核心竞争力的国际化服务经济与前沿创新经济集群，打造一流中央商务区产业生态，建成具有较强世界影响力的现代化国际开放枢纽核心承载区。

三、产业发展重点

（一）提升国际化中央商务区核心功能产业

1. 高能级总部经济

充分释放枢纽区位与开放优势，联动长三角生产制造与产业投资，打造合作共赢的高能级总部集聚升级新高地。重点发展综合型总部、功能型总部、国际组织（机构）总部。

2. 高溢出会展经济

放大进博会溢出效应，强化会展流量型、开放型经济特点，打通国际会展产业链，营造会展经济新生态，建成国际会展之都承载地。聚焦全链发展的国际会展服务、科技引领的智慧会展服务。

3. 高流量贸易经济

构建高端资源配置国际贸易中心新平台，开拓发展新型国际贸易，打造联动长三角、服务全国、辐射亚太的进口商品集散地。聚焦融入全球的数字贸易、特色开放的服务贸易、高效便利的离岸贸易、新生态赋能的供应链服务。

4. 高端化服务经济

推动服务业向国际化、专业化、高端化延伸，打造集枢纽临空服务、科技创新服务、产业金融服务、高端专业服务于一体的现代化专业服务业集聚发展区，全方位服务长三角实体经济发展。聚焦高效联动的临空服务、联通国内国际的科技服务、链接全球的产业金融、集成优质的专业服务。

（二）布局融合创新的未来产业新赛道

1. 数字新经济

以上海城市数字化转型为契机，依托商务区数字场景赋能创新优势，推动商务区数字经济高质量发展，布局打造长三角数字经济创新走廊，成为长三角数字经济创新动力核。聚焦元宇宙、人工智能、工业互联网、电竞游戏、北斗导航等领域。

2. 生命新科技

探索"新医疗、新医药、新医械"一体化医疗融合创新发展模式，积极发展国际医疗高端服务、智慧医疗高端产品、创新药、医疗器械和旅游医疗等特色新赛道，引领国际化医学医疗服务创新。聚焦国际特色医疗服务、生命科学临床转化、国际医药器械贸易、数字健康医疗服务等领域。

3. 低碳新能源

依托全球新能源头部产业集聚的优势，加强创新协同和场景示范，探索布局前沿零碳产业和碳交易服务，打造绿色低碳示范实践区。聚焦新能源产业、前沿零碳产业、碳交易服务产业。

4. 汽车新势力

依托汽车新势力总部研发功能优势，汇聚造车新势力和传统造车企业总部，推动机场、高铁、地铁一体立体化交通智慧出行服务，打造上下游协同创新的智慧新交通产业集群。聚焦新能源汽车、智能网联汽车、智慧交通出行服务。

5. 时尚新消费

依托进博会全球商品首发地和长三角高端消费人群，鼓励国际商品零售、中国品牌孵化和国际品质的文化消费服务，着力打造上海国际大都市内贸外贸相互链接的国际消费新中心。聚焦国际商品零售、中国品牌孵化服务、文旅消费服务。

四、产业发展布局

结合商务区总体发展格局，通过打通片区轴线，优化空间布局，推动产业业态融合发展、片区分工合作发展、长三角产业联动发展，形成核心带动、东西呼应、南北联动的"一圈、四区、三轴"产业空间布局。

（一）一圈：环枢纽核心圈

以虹桥机场高铁综合交通枢纽为中心，重点依托商务区核心区，辐射涵盖虹桥机场东片区、长嘉闵交界区及国家会展中心（上海）连片区，重点发展高能级总部经济、高溢出会展经济、高流量贸易经济、高端化服务经济，营造能级优先、创新先行的中央商务活动区发展氛围，成为商务云集、绿色生态、出行便利的虹桥城市新中心。

（二）四区：产业功能片区

南虹桥片区，以国际化公共服务功能和多元高端融合的服务经济为主要特色。东虹桥片区，以临空枢纽经济和数字服务经济为主要特色，成为国内领先的临空经济示范区。西虹桥片区，以国际化会展经济和北斗数字经济为特色，推动会商数贸融合发展。北虹桥片区，以智慧绿色创新经济与制造服务经济为特色，成为智造创新领航区。

（三）三轴：创新联动发展轴

结合产业项目与区位交通实际，构造"南、中、北"三条产业创新联动发展轴，打通片区产业发展节点，形成产业发展联动合力。

南向"生命科创发展轴"。以闵行前湾地区为起点，经过核心区，沿嘉闵高架路向南延伸，对接G60科创走廊联通南向拓展带，重点布局生命新科技、低碳新能源等产业。

中部"数字干线发展轴"。以长宁天山西路为起点向西经过核心区，沿G50沪渝高速延伸对接青浦长三角数字干线，重点布局数字新经济、时尚新消费等产业。

北向"创新新势力发展轴"。由长宁临空经济示范区为起点，经金沙江西路向西北延伸至嘉定，对接G2京沪高速联通南向拓展带，重点布局汽车新势力、低碳新能源、数字新经济等产业。

五、发展举措

围绕创新产业服务体系、推进功能平台建设、强化关键基础支撑、营造人才集聚生态、打响虹桥整体品牌、推动政策制度创新六大方面，形成各类举措，高质量推进商务区产业创新发展。

附录5：关于支持上海虹桥国际中央商务区进一步提升能级的若干政策措施

商务区是虹桥国际开放枢纽的核心区，是上海服务构建新发展格局、推进落实长三角一体化发展国家战略、全面强化"四大功能"、加快发展"五型经济"的重要承载区，为落实《总体方案》，加快提升虹桥国际中央商务区能级，更好发挥引领带动作用，制定本政策措施。

一、进一步强化"大商务"功能，加快建设一流的国际化中央商务区和开放共享的国际贸易中心新平台

（一）支持跨国公司事业部总部、区域性总部等各种类型总部机构在商务区集聚发展，建立商务区跨国公司地区总部项目储备库，进一步增强跨国公司地区总部投资、销售、采购、研发等核心功能。（责任单位：市商务委、商务区管委会）

（二）设立商务区民营企业总部培育库，鼓励企业加快在商务区集聚业务、拓展功能，升级成为民营企业总部，加快打造长三角民营企业总部集聚区。（责任单位：市经济信息化委、市商务委、市工商联、商务区管委会）

（三）支持商务区内符合条件的企业积极开展离岸经贸业务，进一步扩大离岸经贸企业"白名单"。鼓励商业银行提供基于自由贸易账户的跨境金融服务便利，优化非自由贸易账户离岸贸易资金结算。（责任单位：人民银行上海总部、市商务委、商务区管委会）

（四）在商务区设立线上线下结合的企业"走出去"一站式服务窗口。在虹桥海外贸易中心加挂"上海市'一带一路'综合服务中心"牌子，强化对共建"一带一路"贸易投资促进功能。（责任单位：市发展改革委、市商务委、市贸促会、商务区管委会）

（五）在商务区保税物流中心（B型）优先试点涉检商品集中检验、分批核销工作模式，创新多元化担保机制。（责任单位：上海海关、商务区管委会）

（六）推进新虹桥国际医学中心社会办医与公立医疗机构协同发展，支持公立医疗机构在技术、服务、品牌等方面与新虹桥国际医学中心民营医疗机构开展合作。（责任单位：市卫生健康委、市发展改革委、商务区管委会）

（七）支持虹桥临空经济示范区提升能级，加快虹桥国际机场东片区改造。（责任单位：市发展改革委）

二、持续提升"大会展"能级，更好承接放大进博会溢出带动效应

（一）持续打响会展业"大虹桥"品牌，支持商务区建立会展业发展协调机制和国际会展活动引进、申办联动机制，支持虹桥国际会展产业园提升能级。（责任单位：市商务委、商务区管委会）

（二）制定商务区促进会展经济发展专项政策，支持会展全产业人才培育、标准化体系建设和产业集群发展，为符合条件的会展举办单位、会展服务单位、会展项目以及会展人才提供扶持。（责任单位：商务区管委会、市商务委、市人力资源社会保障局、市财政局）

（三）加大国际知名会展企业总部、境内外专业组展机构、国际品牌重要展会和上下游配套企业引进力度。（责任单位：市商务委、商务区管委会）

三、不断完善"大交通"基础，着力打造联通国际国内的开放枢纽

（一）加快研究商务区中运量公交系统规划，构建内外联动的全域网络，支持近期开通区域内骨干公交线路。（责任单位：市交通委、市发展改革委、商务区管委会）

（二）优化S20外环线和G15沈海高速功能，支持S20外环线抬升辅道及配套路网建设。（责任单位：市交通委、市发展改革委）

（三）支持商务区内区区对接道路建设，进一步完善区域内交通网络。（责任单位：市交通委、市发展改革委、市财政局）

四、着力强化要素支撑和政策保障，进一步提升资源配置功能

（一）支持商务区内符合条件的区域基础性开发项目申报地方政府专项债券。（责任单位：市发展改革委、市财政局）

（二）支持市级新设立的政府出资产业投资基金落户商务区。（责任单位：市发展改革委、商务区管委会）

（三）结合商务区国土空间中近期规划编制工作，"十四五"期间，在不突破规划总量的前提下，按照中心城区建设标准，以设计定高度，以高度定容量，合理确定其核心区域开发强度和容量。（责任单位：市规划资源局、商务区管委会）

（四）"十四五"期间，市级层面对商务区内重大项目土地指标予以优先保障。（责任单位：市规划资源局、商务区管委会）

（五）增加单幅小型商办用地供地，试点实施商住用地动态调整机制，允许按程序将商务区内已建低效商办楼宇改造为保障性租赁住房。（责任单位：市规划资源局、市房屋管理局、商务区管委会）

（六）按照职住平衡原则，通过新建、配建、改建等方式，加快在商务区增加保障性租赁住房供应，主要安排在核心区、轨道交通站点附近、产业园区及周边等区域，在土地供应、规划调整、政策标准等方面给予支持，引导产城人融合、人地房联动。（责任单位：市房屋管理局、市规划资源局、商务区管委会）

（七）强化商务区与虹桥涉外贸易中心等周边区域在政策保障等方面的联动发展。（责任单位：市发展改革委、商务区管委会）

附录6：关于支持上海虹桥国际中央商务区贸易型总部企业发展的若干措施

为贯彻落实《总体方案》（发改地区〔2021〕249号）《虹桥国际开放枢纽中央商务区"十四五"规划》（沪府发〔2021〕14号）和《上海市鼓励企业设立贸易型总部的若干意见》（沪商规〔2021〕5号），深化虹桥国际开放枢纽建设，持续提升区域发展核心功能，高水平打造国际贸易中心新平台，全面服务长三角一体化发展、中国国际进口博览会等国家发展战略，现就支持商务区贸易型总部企业集聚发展提出以下措施。

一、支持贸易型总部企业在商务区集聚发展

本文所称贸易型总部企业，是指境内外企业在商务区设立并注册，具有独立法人资格、开展实体化经营并具有采购、分拨、营销、结算、物流、营运等单一或综合贸易及服务功能，对区域经济社会发展贡献突出的总部机构。

贸易型总部企业由商务区管委会根据商务区贸易产业的发展重点和区域发展实际认定，应当符合以下标准：

（一）申报对象符合本文贸易型总部企业定义；

（二）近三年内未因重大违法违规行为受到税收、安全生产、生态环境等方面行政处罚；

（三）近三年企业法定代表人无刑事犯罪记录或被人民法院列入失信被执行人名单；

（四）营业收入符合以下任一条件：

1. 以国内批发零售为主营业务的，该业务收入占总营业收入的比例占50%以上，且上年度营业收入（销售收入）超过60亿元人民币；

2. 以国际货物贸易为主营业务的，该业务收入占总营业收入的比例占50%以上，且上年度营业收入（销售收入）超过20亿元人民币；

3. 以服务贸易为主营业务的，该业务收入占总营业收入的比例占50%以上，且上年度营业收入（销售收入）超过10亿元人民币；

4. 以平台交易为主营业务的，面向消费者的平台企业年交易额超过30亿元人民币，面向企业（提供企业间交易）的平台企业年交易额超过100亿元人民币。

对商务区打造国际贸易中心新平台和产业发展有重大贡献的企业，经商务区管委会和所在区认定，可适当放宽条件。

注册在商务区内的企业，经行业主管部门按照相关规定，认定为本市贸易型总部企业的，视为商务区贸易型总部企业。

二、支持贸易型总部企业招才引智

（一）健全居住证积分、居转户和直接落户等梯度化人才引进政策体系，支持贸易型总部企业引进所需的高级管理人员、专业技术人才、有特殊贡献者等各类优秀人才。由行业主管部门择优推荐贸易型总部企业纳入上海市人才引进重点机构清单，为其引进的优秀人才落户提供便利。（市人力资源社会保障局、市科委（市外专局）、市商务委、商务区管委会、闵行区政府、长宁区政府、青浦区政府、嘉定区政府）

（二）对贸易型总部企业引进的人才优先提供人才公寓、公共租赁住房、"先租后售"公租房等住房保障服务，并在子女入学、医疗保障等方面提供便利。鼓励各区设立总部人才基金，对贸易型总部的优秀人才予以奖励。（闵行区政府、长宁区政府、青浦区政府、嘉定区政府、商务区管委会）

（三）支持贸易型总部企业符合条件的中国籍人员，因商务需要赴亚太经合组织相关国家，申办APEC商务旅行卡，享受各经济体相互为其商务人员提供的多边长期签证和快速通关礼遇。（市政府外办、上海边检总站）

（四）支持需多次临时入境的贸易型总部企业外籍人员，申请办理入境有效期不超过1年，停留期不超过180日的多次签证。需临时来本市的贸易型总部企业外籍人员，来不及向中国驻外使领馆申请入境签证的，可通过本地出入境管理部门向苏浙皖沪三省一市拟入境口岸的口岸签证机关申请口岸签证入境。［市公安局（市出入境管理局）、市政府外办］

（五）支持贸易型总部企业聘雇的在本市长期居留的外籍人员，按规定申请办理3年至5年有效的外国人居留许可。贸易型总部企业引进的外籍高层次人才经商务区管委会推荐，可以优先申办永久居留。［市公安局（市出入境管理局）、商务区管委会］

（六）上海海关为贸易型总部企业法定代表人及其与总部职能相关的外籍高级管理人员办理健康证明提供绿色通道。（上海海关、商务区管委会）

三、加大对贸易型总部企业金融支持

（一）支持商业银行为贸易型总部企业办理新型离岸国际贸易跨境资金结算业务时，按照"实质重于形式"的要求，根据展业三原则，按规定自主决定审核交易单证的种类。（外汇管理局上海市分局、人民银行上海总部）

（二）支持政策性银行向商务区提供专项信贷额度，运用政策性金融产品支持区内贸易型总部企业扩大进出口贸易、加强企业能力和外贸产业链建设，为商务区加快形成贸易型总部集聚区提供全方位多层次金融服务。（进出口银行上海分行、商务区管委会）

（三）支持政策性保险公司帮助贸易型总部企业用足用好政策性金融工具，提升风险管理能力、完善贸易全链条风险管理机制、开展内外贸一体化、强化支持海外仓和跨境电商等新业态新贸易及促进供应链上下游贸易融资，对贸易型总部企业运用信用政策工具开展上述业务所发生的费用，可根据实际情况由商务区专项资金予以支持，最高不超过企业实际支出的50%。（商务区管委会、中信保上海分公司、闵行区政府、长宁区政府、青浦区政府、嘉定区政府、市财政局）

（四）拓宽贸易型总部企业融资渠道，鼓励更多高能级金融投融资机构集聚虹桥，与贸易型总部企业开展战略性合作，通过统一授信、资产重组、发行债券、引进股权投资等多种方式拓宽贸易融资渠道。鼓励、支持融资租赁公司为贸易型总部企业提供金融服务。鼓励贸易型总部企业向金融机构共享信息，为上下游企业增信，在真实交易的背景下，引导金融机构向贸易型总部企业的上下游企业提供供应链金融产品。（人民银行上海总部、上海银保监局、市地方金融监管局）

四、支持贸易型总部企业提高资金运作和管理能力

（一）支持贸易型总部企业开立自由贸易账户。对有实际离岸经贸业务需求的企业，优先推荐其纳入本市"离岸经贸业务企业名单"。（市商务委、人民银行上海总部、外汇管理局上海市分局、市地方金融监管局）

（二）对内部资金有统一管理需求且符合相关条件的贸易型总部企业，支持其所在企业集团或外商投资性公司按照有关规定申报设立财务公司，为其成员单位提供集中

财务管理服务。（上海银保监局、市地方金融监管局）

（三）鼓励贸易型总部企业根据自身经营和管理需要，开展各类跨境人民币业务。支持符合条件的贸易型总部企业设立在岸的全功能型跨境人民币资金池，开展集团内跨境资金集中管理，允许境外成员企业与区内的主办企业之间或境外主办企业与区内成员企业之间自行选择货币进行资金归集。（人民银行上海总部）

（四）支持符合条件的贸易型总部企业按照跨国公司跨境资金集中运营管理规定，申请开展跨境资金集中运营业务，集中运营管理境内外资金，办理经常项目资金集中收付和轧差净额结算以及外债和境外放款额度集中管理等。（人民银行上海总部、外汇管理局上海市分局）

（五）外汇管理部门加强对贸易型总部企业的指导服务。商务区管委会优先向试点银行推荐贸易型总部企业参与贸易外汇收支便利化试点，对符合条件的企业，试点银行可实施以下便利化措施：优化单证审核；货物贸易超期限等特殊退汇业务免于事前登记；货物贸易对外付汇时免于办理进口报关单核验手续；服务贸易项下非关联关系的境内外机构间发生的代垫或分摊或超12个月的代垫或分摊业务，由试点银行审核真实性、合理性后办理。（外汇管理局上海市分局、商务区管委会）

五、支持贸易型总部企业提升贸易规模

（一）加强对贸易型总部企业海关信用培育，将符合条件的贸易型总部企业优先纳入重点培育企业名单，优先培育，优先认证，成为高级认证企业后享受AEO通关便利。（上海海关）

（二）支持符合条件的贸易型总部企业申请认定中国国际进口博览会上海交易团"6天+365天"交易服务平台。支持和推荐符合条件的贸易型总部企业申请上海市国际贸易分拨中心示范企业评定。（市商务委、商务区管委会、闵行区政府、长宁区政府、青浦区政府、嘉定区政府）

（三）加大出口退税等政策支持力度，对符合条件的贸易型总部企业在国内采购并运往境外作为投资或用于工程项下的货物，按规定办理出口退税。依托长三角区域一体化协作机制，推动实现长三角区域内出口退（免）税企业分类管理评定结果互认。对迁入商务区的符合认定条件的贸易型总部企业，税务部门将建立重点联系制度，并适用迁入前原评定的出口退（免）税管理类别相应的管理服务举措，便利其办理出口退（免）税。优先推荐符合条件的贸易型总部企业列入上海全面数字化的电子发票试

点。（市税务局）

（四）鼓励符合条件的贸易型总部企业申请认定技术先进型服务企业，对经认定的技术先进型服务企业，减按15%的税率征收企业所得税。（市科委、市税务局、市商务委）

（五）支持上海国际贸易"单一窗口"为商务区贸易型总部企业提供通关、金融、供应链等跨境贸易便利化及数字化服务，帮助商务区贸易型总部企业享受国际贸易协定优惠措施，进一步为国际贸易赋能。（市商务委、亿通公司）

六、支持贸易型总部企业拓展国际市场

（一）建立和完善区内支持贸易型总部企业"走出去"服务体系，加快引进和培育对外投资专业人才和专业服务机构，充分发挥各类公共服务平台和行业协会作用，加强国际经贸领域供需双方信息对接。（市商务委、市发展改革委、商务区管委会）

（二）加强国际经贸市场运行分析和预警，强化企业"走出去"的贸易摩擦应对和贸易投资合规指导，帮助企业提升风险防范意识和能力。（市商务委、市发展改革委、商务区管委会）

（三）支持对贸易型总部企业开展境外投资合作业务所得，按规定实施盈亏弥补及税收直接、间接饶让抵免等税收政策。（市税务局）

七、完善贸易型总部企业服务机制

（一）商务区管委会对认定的贸易型总部企业，给予营运专项补贴和人才专项补贴，补贴标准和资金渠道参照虹桥国际中央商务区关于支持内资总部企业发展的政策意见执行。（商务区管委会、闵行区政府、长宁区政府、青浦区政府、嘉定区政府、市财政局）

（二）建立贸易型总部企业服务专员对接机制，提供"一对一"企业全生命周期的定制化服务；支持贸易型总部企业参加中国国际进口博览会，并为其提供便利化服务。将贸易型总部企业纳入本市政企合作圆桌会议机制。发挥"上海市企业服务云"、上海市民营企业总部服务中心和长三角民营企业总部服务中心作用，为贸易型总部企业提供精准服务。（商务区管委会、市商务委、市经济信息化委、市工商联、闵行区政府、长宁区政府、青浦区政府、嘉定区政府）

附录7：上海虹桥国际中央商务区关于支持内资总部企业发展的政策意见

为进一步贯彻《总体方案》（发改地区〔2021〕249号）、《上海市鼓励设立民营企业总部的若干意见》（沪商规〔2019〕1号）等要求，加快集聚内资总部企业，构筑商务区总部经济集聚升级新高地，依据《上海市虹桥商务区专项发展资金管理办法》及其实施细则，特制定本政策意见。

一、支持重点

支持工商注册地、实地经营地和税收户管地均在商务区（151.4平方千米范围内）的内资总部企业发展。鼓励符合条件的企业申请上海市相关总部，支持符合条件的企业申报商务区综合型企业总部和功能型企业总部，并对符合条件的国际商务合作伙伴予以支持，进一步增强商务区总部经济活力。具体包括：

（一）经上海市相关总部认定办法，取得贸易型总部、民营企业总部的，视为商务区综合型企业总部；取得民营企业总部型机构的，视为商务区功能型企业总部。

（二）经商务区管委会认定的综合型企业总部和功能型总部。

1. 综合型企业总部

具有独立法人资格，以投资或授权形式对相应的区域内2家及以上分支机构行使管理和服务职能的总部性质企业。重点支持本土跨国公司、央企第二总部、长三角总部企业。

2. 功能型企业总部

经母公司（集团）授权，承担集团内相应区域分支机构管理决策、资金管理、采购、销售、物流、结算、研发、培训等一项或多项总部功能的独立法人企业。

（三）国际商务合作伙伴

经商务区认定的致力于共同打造虹桥国际开放枢纽、做强商务区总部能级的国内外知名决策咨询机构、专业服务机构、投资促进机构，以及国际级组织、高能级商协会组织等第三方机构。

二、主要支持内容

（一）营运专项补贴

支持综合型企业总部和功能型企业总部做强行业引领功能，不断提高行业显示度，两年内给予其营运专项补贴。其中综合型企业总部最高不超过3 000万元人民币，功能型企业总部最高不超过1 500万元人民币。

（二）能级提升补贴

鼓励综合型企业总部开展并购整合资源做强做大。对经有关部门认定的有效并购重组事项，依据其并购前期费用的50%，给予其最高不超过200万元人民币并购专项补贴。

鼓励功能型企业总部升级为综合型总部机构，对于实现能级提升的，给予其最高不超过500万元人民币的能级专项补贴。

（三）人才发展支持

鼓励综合型企业总部和功能型企业总部大力吸引专业性、国际化、创新型人才，给予最高不超过200万元人民币的人才专项补贴。

对上述人才，给予其落户以及人才公寓等支持，并为外籍高层次人才提供签证、居留、永久居留等便利。

（四）国际商务合作支持

支持国际商务合作伙伴充分放大商务区大商务、大会展、大交通融合发展优势，开展国际化、高层次的高端商务活动，引领带动一批高质量总部企业集聚商务区，全面提升商务区高端资源配置能力和辐射引领能力。经认定，对于国际商务合作伙伴举办的高端商务活动给予其最高不超过100万元人民币的支持；并依据其年度总部企业带动落地情况，给予每年最高不超过200万元人民币的支持。

三、附则

1. 本意见由商务区管委会负责解释。

2. 本意见实施过程中如遇国家或者本市颁布新政策，则按相关规定执行。对已享受其他市级或者区级财政扶持政策的项目，专项资金不再重复支持。

3. 本意见所指总部企业的申报认定以及政策支持细则等，以年度申报指南为准。

4. 本意见实施后，《上海虹桥商务区促进现代服务业发展的政策意见》第四条第十三款重点引进项目的装修补贴政策不再执行。

5. 国际商务合作伙伴享受本政策高端商务活动支持的，《上海虹桥商务区促进现代服务业发展的政策意见》第四条第二款第三点活动补贴不再享受。

6. 本实施意见自发布之日起实施，有效期至2023年12月31日。

Chapter I   Economic "Stable Growth"

Section One   Background Situation

I. International level

In 2022, the global economic situation and geopolitical pattern have undergone profound changes. No matter from the perspective of regional distribution, cyclical evolution trend or supply and demand structure, the downward pressure on the global economy is increasing, and the economic growth is slowing down quarter by quarter. The COVID–19 has a far-reaching impact. The risk of economic downturn in major economies in the world has increased, the risk of global stagflation has increased, and policy contraction in major economies has accelerated. At the same time, crises and opportunities coexist, the global scientific and technological and industrial revolution accelerates, technological progress and industrial upgrading continue to evolve, green transformation and sustainable development are in the ascendant, and the global economy is in a critical period of transformation of old and new drivers and structural adjustment.

The impact of the COVID-19 on the global value chain and international trade will remain a prominent problem to global trade in the future. The trade decline of industries characterized by complex value chain linkages, especially the electronic and automotive products industries, may be greater. The epidemic has caused the global industrial chain and supply chain to face the crisis of chain breakage. Multinational companies have paid more attention to seeking the reconstruction of the supply chain of proximity and localization, and promoted the "more permanent change" of the industrial chain layout. The epidemic has promoted the combination of the Internet, big data and traditional foreign trade industries, accelerated the digitization process of service trade, and promoted the diversification of trade patterns.

The restructuring of the global economic and trade system is accelerating. At present, the trend of anti-globalization is on the rise, unilateralism and protectionism are on the rise, and the world has entered a new period of turbulence and change. The India-Pacific Economic Framework (IPEF) led by the United States and the European Union's Global Gateway plan have been introduced in succession. High-standard economic and trade agreements such as the Comprehensive and Progressive Trans-Pacific Partnership Agreement (CPTPP) and the Digital Economic Partnership Agreement (DEPA) have become new demands for national/regional development. In the long run, Sino-US trade relations will be in the game process of competition and cooperation for a long time, and enter into "comprehensive competition with management"; China-Russia and China-EU relations are increasingly important and complex, and China-EU cooperation in digital transformation and green development has broad prospects in the future.

A new round of industrial reform reshapes the industrial competition landscape. At present, the new round of industrial transformation, which is booming in the world, is led by the maturity, diffusion and deep integration of a group of general technologies with information technology as the core, and has a profound impact on the production mode, market mode and enterprise organization relationship built in the era of industrial production. The developed countries have a strong intention to rely on basic technologies to control the competitiveness of emerging industries. In the fields of information, energy, environment, biology, manufacturing, ocean, space and other industries, the United States controls most basic technologies. Under the new situation of the new round of industrial reform, the market size of the demand-side, the diversified composition of the demand-side, and the differentiated level of the demand content determine the development space of emerging industries. The new round of industrial transformation has the characteristics of digital and intelligent technology, which makes the cost economy of replacing labor with advanced technology and equipment gradually apparent, and may reshape the world industrial competition landscape.

II. National level

Opening up to the outside world is an important driving force for China's economic and social development. Promoting reform and development through opening up is an important weapon for China's development to make new achievements. President Xi attached great importance to the work of opening up to the outside world, clearly pointed out that opening up is a distinctive symbol of contemporary China, and stressed that "the door of China's opening up will not be closed, but will only be wider and wider". In the video speech at the opening ceremony of the fifth China Import and Export Expo in 2022, it was also pointed out that openness is an important driving force for the progress of human civilization and the only way for the prosperity and development of the world. In the report of the 20th National Congress of the Communist Party of China, it was pointed out that "we should promote the high-level opening up. Relying on the advantages of China's super-scale market, we should attract global resource elements through the domestic circulation, enhance the linkage effect of the two resources in the domestic and international markets, and improve the quality and level of trade and investment cooperation. We should steadily expand the institutional opening of rules, regulations, management, standards and other systems".

In 2022, China's COVID-19 epidemic repeatedly impact the economy from both supply and demand. Expectations weakened, the economic environment changed dramatically, and downward pressure increased sharply. The difficulty of epidemic prevention and control was greater than that in 2020. It is more difficult to coordinate epidemic prevention and control and economic and social development. The difficulties of enterprise production and operation are more prominent. In the face of these difficulties and challenges, the domestic epidemic prevention policy has been continuously optimized, helping enterprises to bail out, expanding domestic demand, and stabilizing growth policy has been continuously strengthened. The moderate and controllable price level provides sufficient space for the flexible operation of macro policies, and exports still have strong support. With the gradual effectiveness of these policies and measures, the economy will continue to resume its development trend.

The development of foreign trade has made remarkable achievements, with remarkable achievements in the introduction of foreign capital and foreign investment. In the face of the complex changing domestic and international situation and the impact of the COVID-19, China's foreign trade still showed strong resilience and comprehensive competitiveness, and achieved rapid stability. In 2020, China's total trade in goods and services ranked first in the world and became the world's largest trading country, with an international market share of 14.7%. At the same time, the trade structure has been continuously optimized, mechanical and electrical products and high-tech products have become the main body of export, and private enterprises have become the main force of foreign trade. Significant achievements have been made in the development of foreign investment and foreign investment. In 2021, China's foreign investment broke the trillion-yuan mark for the first time, reaching a record high, which is the first time to achieve double-digit growth in nearly 10 years. According to the 2021 World Investment Report, China has become the world's second largest foreign direct investment inflow country and the first largest foreign direct investment country. At the same time, from the positive list to the negative list management, from the "Three Laws on Foreign Investment" to the "Foreign Investment Law", China's opening door is opening wider and wider, and is becoming a hot spot for many foreign investments.

III. Yangtze River Delta integration level

2022 is the fourth year for the Yangtze River Delta integration to become a national strategy. The Yangtze River Delta, which accounts for 4% of the country's total economic output, is one of the most active, open and innovative regions in China. In the past four years, Shanghai, Jiangsu, Zhejiang and Anhui have taken frequent actions, each of which has its own strengths and coordinated efforts, and the two key points-"integration" and "high quality" have been closely followed to create a strong and active growth pole, accelerate the rise of industrial clusters, and achieve fruitful results in the construction of integration demonstration zones.

The Yangtze River Delta has accelerated the process of high-quality economic development. As of August 2022, the number of specialized, special and new enterprises in Shanghai, Ningbo and Suzhou ranked the 2nd, 4th and 10th in the country respectively. The main industries focused on general equipment manufacturing, electronic information manufacturing, software information services, biomedicine, high-end equipment manufacturing and other fields, forming a relatively stable upstream and downstream cooperation relationship in the industrial chain. The specialized, special and new enterprises can improve the development level of regional manufacturing industry and enhance the resilience of the industrial chain supply chain. At present, in order to solve the problems of supply chain security, some enterprises in the Yangtze River Delta are planning to implement the "business diversification strategy", and actively seeking the "China+1" or "China+2" business backup center. The complex external environment that the cities in the Yangtze River Delta are facing is common. We need to give full play to the overall advantages, let the industrial chain gears accurately mesh, build the common market in the Yangtze River Delta, make full use of domestic demand-oriented and internally recyclable articles, and work together to create a new highland of reform and opening up.

The "Fourteenth Five-Year Plan" outlines the integrated development landscape. The "Fourteenth Five-Year Plan" of the Yangtze River Delta Integrated Development Plan has defined 22 major policies, 104 major issues and 16 major projects. It is proposed that by 2025, the Yangtze River Delta integrated development will make substantial progress, the system and mechanism for integrated development will be fully established, and the integration development of key regional sectors such as cross-border regions, urban and rural areas will reach a high level, and the scientific and creative industries, collaborative opening, infrastructure, ecological environment, public services and other fields have basically achieved integration. It has made detailed planning from the following aspects: taking the lead in building a new development pattern, promoting the coordinated development of key regions, accelerating the construction of a collaborative innovation industrial system, promoting a higher level of collaborative opening, strengthening infrastructure connectivity, jointly building a green and beautiful Yangtze River Delta, sharing higher quality public services, innovating the integrated development system and mechanism, building a high-level security Yangtze River Delta and security measures, and proposed to play the role of new media Integrate media resources and tell the "Yangtze River Delta story" well.

IV. Shanghai level

Since the 18th National Congress of the Communist Party of China, Shanghai has unswervingly adhered to the expansion of opening up, guided by the implementation of major national strategic tasks, and formed a large number of innovative reforms, leading opening up, and pioneering innovation, and has become a highland for all-round and high-level opening up. Actively implement the strategy of expanding domestic demand, promote the quality and capacity of consumption, and the total retail sales of consumer goods doubled, leaping to the first place in the country. Give play to the decisive role of the market in the allocation of resources, promote the smooth flow of commodity elements and resources in a wider range, multiply the number of commodity trading platforms with the scale of 10 billion and 100 billion, and make important breakthroughs in the construction of modern commercial circulation system. At the same time, promote the high-quality development of trade, the function of trade hub has been continuously enhanced, and the global market share has continued to increase as the largest trade port city in the world.

Hongqiao International Central Business District focuses on promoting high-quality economic development, accelerating the agglomeration of headquarter-based economy, accelerating the formation of high-value-added, high-growth, high-energy industrial clusters, and steady development of flow-based economy. The "one core" drive is stronger, and the "two belts" construction highlights are numerous. The "Hongqiao function" serves the new development pattern. The three core functions of big transportation, big exhibition and big business are continuously highlighted, the international positioning is further strengthened, and the global resource allocation capacity is significantly enhanced. "Hongqiao Speed" leads high-quality development. As the core bearing area of Hongqiao International Open Hub, Hongqiao International Central Business District will see a year-on-year increase of 20.9% in tax revenue in the first quarter of 2022, which is 10.7 percentage points faster than the average growth rate of the city; The total amount of investment and construction projects attracted in 2022 is nearly 120 billion yuan, up 60% from last year. "Hongqiao Duty" helped win the Great Shanghai Epidemic Prevention Action. In the current round of the epidemic prevention test, "Great Hongqiao" strengthened the cooperation between water, land and air. Hongqiao Airport and Hongqiao Railway Station fully served the "big forces" to aid Shanghai. The "four-leaf grass" of the National Convention and Exhibition Center became the main force in the shelter, fully exerting the hub connectivity function and resource allocation capability. At the same time, the six districts of "Dahongqiao" have coordinated the epidemic prevention and control and economic and social development, orderly promoted the resumption of work and production, and rapidly implemented the corporate rescue policy, laying a solid foundation for accelerating the economic recovery and revitalization.

The next five years will be a critical period for the beginning of the comprehensive construction of a modern socialist country. One of the main objectives and tasks is to basically form a new system of an open economy with a higher level. As the core of the functional layout of Hongqiao International Open Hub, the next five years will also be a key window period for this 151.4 square kilometers area to strive to build the core functions of the world-class CBD. Hongqiao International Central Business District will give better play to its geographical and geographical advantages, create an international business environment, improve the comprehensive capacity of comprehensive government public services, undertake the mission of a higher level of openness, form a relatively independent urban form, and better carry the headquarters economy and flow economy.

Section Three   Investment Promotion

I. Organize and carry out a series of activities of investment.

Since the second half of 2021, the management committee has formed an upsurge of attracting investment through three major activities, such as signing contracts in batches, breakfast meetings for entrepreneurs, and "Ride The Wave of Rising Shanghai" investing in Hongqiao. During the epidemic in the first half of 2022, the management committee held a series of investment promotion online meetings, and enterprise symposiums in different industries to actively help enterprises solve operational difficulties and strengthen the role of business promotion.

Focusing on the theme of "Ride The Wave of Rising Shanghai" investment in Shanghai global sharing season, we have constantly expanded the circle of friends for investment attraction, and carried out cooperation with business associations, professional institutions, and international business partners. Through the combination of online and offline activities, we have carried out more than 30 activities (including 18 online activities, attracting a total of 310000 online participants), We have successively held investment promotion activities such as the "Ride The Wave of Rising Shanghai, Come Together Online at Hongqiao" - Hongqiao International CBD Development Opportunity Presentation Conference and the new situation of international trade and enterprise response, "Ride The Wave of Rising Shanghai, Come Together Online at Hongqiao" - Hongqiao International CBD Development Opportunity Presentation Conference (Switzerland special session), and the "Ride The Wave of Rising Shanghai, Investment in Hongqiao -New ideas of the stock of the great changes in asset management" to talk about the asset management opportunity forum, 2022 The 10th China Automotive and Environmental Innovation Forum and the 14th Global Automotive Industry Summit and other thematic summit forums, the RCEP enterprise service special session (seize the opportunity to make good use of the effective dividend of RCEP), the FIEs Community @ Hongqiao digital economy rules and the development opportunities of foreign-funded enterprises and other enterprise development lectures, covering finance, industry, physical Internet, international trade, foreign investment and other fields, Broadly gather the consensus of international business partners to build a new round of development advantages of Hongqiao International CBD.

Tracking and docking more than 200 key projects, forming a digital new economic cluster represented by Wansheng Huaxing, Baiqiu Shangmei, etc; Low-carbon new energy clusters represented by Trina Solar and Jingke Energy; New life science and technology clusters represented by Neusoft Medical and Xinda Biology; New auto force clusters represented by Bosch, Michelin, etc; The brand new consumer clusters represented by Guoquan, Hutou Bureau, etc. will create a good business situation where thousands of businesses gather, elements gather, and multiple intersection, and further improve the overall brand of Hongqiao.

II. Carefully implement the Hongqiao International Business Partnership Initiative.

In order to accelerate the construction of the Hongqiao International Open Hub and increase the overall promotion of the Hongqiao International CBD, in the window period of the national strategy and accelerated economic recovery policy are superimposed, on September 14, the Management Committee held the launch of the "Ride The Wave of Rising Shanghai, Investment in Hongqiao" Hongqiao International Business Partnership Initiative. Wu Qing, member of the Standing Committee of the Municipal Party Committee and Executive Deputy Mayor, Zong Ming, Deputy Mayor, Gu Honghui, Deputy Secretary-General of the Municipal Government, Hua Yuan, Deputy Secretary-General of the Municipal Government and other relevant leaders and enterprise representatives attended the event. At the event, Bao Bingzhang, secretary of the Party Leadership Group and executive deputy director of the Hongqiao International Central Business District Management Committee, made the keynote presentation of "Sharing Opportunities when Ride The Wave of Rising Shanghai, Investing in Hongqiao and Creating the Future", Gu Jun, director of the Municipal Commission of Commerce, issued the policy of Hongqiao's trade-oriented headquarters and private headquarters, Zhang Hongtao, chief engineer of the Municipal Commission of Economic and Information Technology, issued the "Industrial Development

Plan of Hongqiao International Central Business District", and Chen Huawen, head of Minhang District, issued the development plan of Hongqiao Qianwan, Gu Honghui, Deputy Secretary-General of the Municipal Government, and Hua Yuan, Deputy Secretary-General of the Municipal Government, jointly launched the Hongqiao Online New Economic Eco-Park. Zong Ming, Deputy Mayor, issued certificates for the newly recognized headquarter enterprises representatives. Wu Qing, Member of the Standing Committee of the Municipal Party Committee and Executive Vice Mayor, set sail for the Hongqiao International Business Partnership Initiative.

The Hongqiao International Central Business District will take the opportunity of the "Ride The Wave of Rising Shanghai" series activities, carefully implement the Hongqiao International Business Partnership Plan, and establish long-term and stable partnerships with 36 international and high-energy well-known enterprises (associations) such as KPMG and ManpowerGroup, focusing on international professional services, international trade promotion, international financial investment and international industrial agglomeration, to achieve coordinated development and win-win cooperation, We will accelerate the cultivation and expansion of new drivers of development and strive to build new advantages for future development.

III. Make good use of the new mode of "1+1+4+X" investment promotion linkage.

In order to enlarge the function of Hongqiao International Central Business District as a strong and active growth pole in the Yangtze River Delta and the "Rainbow Bridge" function of connecting international and domestic enterprises, further establish the "Hongqiao Opportunity" brand, and use the functional advantages of the business district connecting international enterprises to help the international development of enterprises in the Yangtze River Delta.

Since September 2022, under the leadership of the Management Committee, the government of Minhang District, Changning District, Qingpu District, Jiading District and the real estate Hongqiao District have been linked, giving full play to the "1+1+4+X" investment promotion linkage mechanism, innovating the new model of "going out" promotion and research for regional linkage cooperation, and successfully held the "collaborative development and creating the future" - the Yangtze River Delta Entrepreneur Roundtable in Hefei, Hangzhou and Nanjing, attracting more than 100 enterprises from the Yangtze River Delta to participate in the conference.

Bao Bingzhang, Secretary of the Party Leadership Group and Executive Deputy Director of the Management Committee of Hongqiao International CBD, made a keynote speech, Kong Fu'an, Deputy Director of the Management Committee of Hongqiao International CBD, made a keynote presentation, and leaders of each district made a keynote speech, and invited experts from Bank of China, China Construction Bank, Bank of Communications, Ernst & Young, Manpower, KPMG and other professional service institutions shared international development topics. The participating enterprises had full exchanges and interactions at the meeting, and expressed strong interest in the development of the business district. The promotion activities are intended to give full play to the comprehensive enabling role of Hongqiao in the international development of enterprises, focusing on the "going out" of private enterprises with international development needs in the Yangtze River Delta, and further transform, upgrade and innovate based on the business district.

Chapter II   Construction of Hongqiao International Open Hub

Since the release of the "Overall Plan", according to the work deployment of the municipal party committee and the municipal government, and under the guidance of the municipal coordination and promotion mechanism, the Hongqiao International CBD has comprehensively promoted 29 policy measures (26 have been implemented) of the "Overall Plan", effectively releasing the vitality of the policy and improving the comprehensive competitiveness of the overall regional development. At the same time, with the help of the "Overall Plan" policy, the Hongqiao International CBD, as the "one core", has achieved a good momentum of development, the regional core functions have been further strengthened, the institutional framework and policy system have been further improved, and the support and linkage services in the Yangtze River Delta have been further strengthened.

Section One   Overall Design

The Hongqiao International CBD firmly grasps the major opportunities, strengthens the overall design, and lays a solid foundation for the future development. Focusing on the requirements of "one platform, three tasks, four functions, and five types of economy", it focuses on the global and the future, and targets the highest standards and the best level. It proposes that by 2035, the gross regional product will strive to increase from 140 billion yuan to 600 billion yuan, and the tax revenue will increase from 34.6 billion yuan to 150 billion yuan, and strive to reach 200 billion yuan; Looking forward to 2050, the Hongqiao

International CBD will focus on the overall design from the planning system, institutional system, industrial system and other aspects to form a superimposed effect and gradually play a role in promoting economic development.

I. Organize the preparation of the medium−term and short−term planning of the land space of the Hongqiao International CBD

Based on the above strategic positioning and goal vision, a special class was set up to start the preparation of the medium-term and short-term planning of the land space of the Hongqiao International CBD, and to study and sort out the future planning scheme and spatial layout. At the same time, the Hongqiao International CBD anchors the development outline and overall plan of the Yangtze River Delta integration and implement the strategic requirements of the central government's "three major tasks" and "four major functions" for Shanghai, gives full play to the pivotal role of the two sectors of the internal and external, further clarifies the development plan of the Hongqiao International CBD based on the two nodes of 2035 and 2050, creates a space system of global linkage and cluster development, and strengthen the radiative driving effect of the core area and the main and sub-centers, builds an innovative and collaborative network, a public transport network, an open and dynamic network, and a blue-green space network, and forms five functional blocks with complete functions, distinctive features, and connectivity, so as to achieve a blueprint to govern the whole area and set up four pillars for future development.

II. Promote the formulation of regulations to promote the development of Hongqiao International CBD

After more than ten years of development and construction, the Hongqiao International CBD has moved from construction to a stage where both construction and function building are equally important. Multiple national strategies are superimposed, and it is urgent to formulate relevant local laws and regulations. Define the functional orientation, promotion mechanism and institutional system of the Hongqiao International CBD in the form of legislation, provide legal guarantee for the development of the Hongqiao International CBD, and promote open cooperation in a deeper and broader field with greater efforts. In 2021, this work was included in the key legislative research project of the Municipal People's Congress, and the Hongqiao International CBD Management Committee set up a research group. This year, it also went deep into the units of each district and the frontline of enterprise parks to carry out special research, widely listened to policy appeals and suggestions, and repeatedly studied, demonstrated and revised and improved. The Finance and Economic Commission of the Municipal People's Congress and the Legal Working Committee of the Standing Committee of the Municipal People's Congress gave comprehensive guidance to form the Regulations of Shanghai Municipality on Promoting the Development of Hongqiao International Central Hongqiao International CBD (first draft), Define the functional orientation, promotion mechanism and institutional system of the Hongqiao International CBD, solidify the policy into law, promote reform and institutional innovation under the premise of the rule of law, and provide direct legal basis for the Hongqiao International CBD to administer according to law. In January 2022, the Legislative Research on the Administrative Regulations of Hongqiao Hongqiao International CBD was awarded the "Second Prize" by the Office of the Municipal Committee for the Comprehensive Rule of Law.

This work has also been highly valued by the municipal party committee, the municipal people's congress and the municipal government. With the full support of the then Secretary Li Qiang, Mayor Gong Zheng and Director Jiang Zhuoqing successively held special meetings to study the legislative work of the Regulations, and made clear instructions on the important provisions of the draft. On October 28, the Regulation of Shanghai Municipality on Promoting the Development of Hongqiao International Central Hongqiao International CBD was reviewed and adopted by the Standing Committee of the Shanghai Municipal People's Congress, and came into force on November 1, 2022. The Regulations have nine chapters and sixty-nine articles, which are divided into general principles, regional planning and layout, international business services, new platform of international trade center, comprehensive transportation hub, integration of industry and city, integrated development of service Yangtze River Delta, service and guarantee and supplementary provisions. Its main features include four aspects：First, it highlights the political position and strengthens the implementation of the national strategy with the guarantee of the rule of law. The second is to highlight function building and build a landmark area for reform and opening up in the new era. Third, we should highlight coordinated opening up and help build a new development pattern of domestic and international double circulation. Fourth, highlight the role of the main body and optimize the system and mechanism to form a working force.

III. Compile industrial planning to lead the "four high and five new" industries to accelerate the agglomeration

Focus on the high-energy headquarters economy, high-overflow exhibition economy, high-flow trade economy and high-end service economy with good development foundation and future prospects, lay out and build five new tracks of digital new economy, life new technology, low-carbon new energy, automobile new power, and fashion new consumption, and build the "four high and five new" industrial system. In combination with the "Fourteenth Five-Year Plan" of the Hongqiao International CBD, the "Hongqiao International Central Business District Industrial Development Plan" is prepared around the "3+6" leading industry in Shanghai and the requirements for the development of the "five oriented economy". It is proposed that by 2025, Strive to build the "four high and five new" industrial system (i.e., high-energy headquarters economy, high-spillover exhibition economy, high-flow trade economy, high-end service economy; digital new economy, new life technology, low-carbon new energy, new power of automobile, and new consumption of fashion), and make regular rolling adjustments to achieve the "4311" industrial development goal by 2025. In the future, we will focus on building high-flow trade economy, high-end service economy Four 100-billion-level industrial ecological clusters of digital new economy and fashion new consumption; Build three 50 billion level industries, namely, new life technology, new automobile power and low-carbon new energy; Hold 100 international exhibitions, with international exhibitions accounting for more than 80% and international conferences accounting for more than 25% of the city; The number of enterprises with integrated headquarters and functional headquarters has reached 1000. The industrial planning clarifies the industrial development objectives, industrial positioning and key areas, optimizes the industrial spatial layout, carries out research on supporting policies, and provides guidance for the industrial development, project investment attraction and landing of the Hongqiao International CBD during the "14th Five-Year Plan" period.

In addition, the Hongqiao International CBD has also actively implemented and promoted a number of innovative policies and measures. Comprehensively promote the implementation of the Overall Plan, and around the 29 policies of the Overall Plan, 26 have been implemented, and a number of implementation rules and application cases have been introduced and promoted. We fully implemented the 23 policies of the municipal government to support the further upgrading of the Hongqiao International CBD, formulated and implemented the incentive policies to promote the development of trade-based headquarters and private headquarters, and established a regional statistical cooperation system with the municipal bureau of statistics and the four district governments, leading the supporting role to gradually emerge. Under the leadership of the Municipal Development and Reform Commission, the policy for the construction of Hongqiao International Open Hub 2.0 upgrade is being studied and formulated, and the relevant national departments are being promoted to introduce a number of policies and measures with high content and strong innovation at the "second anniversary".

Section Two   Focus on Building an International CBD

Adhere to the two keys of "integration" and "high quality", accelerate the in-depth integration of high-end business, exhibition and transportation functions, accelerate the development of modern service industry, and build an international CBD with high standards.

Strengthen the core functions of the international exhibition capital. Relying on the National Convention and Exhibition Center and giving full play to the role of the Shanghai Convention and Exhibition Industry Association, the Hongqiao International Convention and Exhibition Industrial Park has been built, attracting nearly 200 enterprises related to the exhibition industry chain, including Yunshang Convention and Exhibition, Infirman, China Trade Macalline and so on. Study the high-quality development path of exhibitions under the normal situation of epidemic prevention and control, and promote the effective combination of traditional exhibitions and digital exhibitions.

Build a centralized exhibition place for the achievements of the Expo. In accordance with the principle of "government guidance, market players, policy support and multi-party linkage", we will build a number of commodity direct sales platforms, national commodity trading centers and professional trade platforms for countries and regions along the "the Belt and Road".

Promote the development of Hongqiao Products to online platform and professional trading platform. Building A of Hongqiao Pinhui has been fully invested, attracting 5700 brands and more than 60000 goods from more than 90 countries and regions to settle and sell, and accelerating the construction of an import goods distribution center linking the Yangtze River Delta, serving the whole country and radiating the Asia-Pacific region. The platform supports the introduction of Jinbaohui live broadcast cross-border e-commerce base, which has 59 live broadcast rooms, focusing on "live+import", "live+bonded", and "live+industry". It is the first batch of live broadcast e-commerce demonstration bases in Shanghai, providing services such as KOL and KCL anchors, video production, content creation, platform distribution, live training, etc., creating an online new economy platform with import as the theme, and broadening the domestic sales channels of imported goods. Deepen the Hongqiao International Coffee Port, gather the coffee industry chain enterprises of "from seed to cup", have introduced more than 30 upstream and downstream coffee enterprises, and more than 20 registered enterprises, realizing a trade volume of 2 billion yuan, and will create a 10 billion level coffee import.

Deepen the characteristics of the National Pavilion of Greenfield Global Commodity Trade Port and the construction of the sub-platform of Hongqiao Overseas Trade Center, and achieve the entry of high-energy tourists through docking with embassies, consulates general and business associations of various countries. In terms of new national embassies, the platform has initially reached the intention of entry with consulates of Iceland, Hungary, Peru, Kazakhstan and other countries; In terms of the upgrading of national pavilions, Thailand, Sri Lanka, Afghanistan and other national pavilions have further expanded their area and categories. It has attracted 180 enterprises and organizations from 76 countries and regions to settle in, set up 61 national pavilions, and introduced more than 90000 imported goods, covering more than 20 major categories, including food and wine, digital home appliances, beauty care, clothing bags, furniture and home furnishing, among which more than 20000 items were imported from the Expo.

To build a brand of "Yuanqi Hongqiao · Global GO", give full play to the role of the Expo in promoting the steady growth of consumption, and guide the spillover effect of the Expo to focus on undertaking platform enterprises to actively carry out the theme promotion activities of the Expo. For example, Hongqiao Pinhui launched a series of activities such as Coffee Culture Week, National Colorful Month, Sake Culture Festival and so on, and launched the brand of "Import to Hongqiao, Consumer Experience to Pinhui"; Greenfield Global Commodity Trade Port launched "G-Hub Global Country Colorful Shopping" in combination with national customs, arts and humanities, food and wine, and launched online and offline interactive experience activities such as the World Beer Festival, the Middle

East Exotic Commodity Exhibition, Türkiye Contemporary Photography Art Exhibition, and Karlov Jewelry Festival through all channels; Through the "live high shopping season", Jinbaohui shows Hongqiao high-quality imported goods to consumers across the country, and increases the awareness of online target consumer groups on the Jinbao Expo and Hongqiao cross-border commodity resources.

Support for the promotion of innovation policies to the Expo to institutionalized arrangements. During the Expo, 19 innovation policies formed a normalized arrangement. At the same time, we actively studied the extension of innovation policies during the Expo to internationally renowned exhibitions with import as the theme in batches and the "6+365 days" perennial exhibition and marketing platform to strengthen the exhibition spillover linkage. Innovative policies such as "protection to exhibition", "exhibition to protection" and "exhibition to cross" have been implemented, and "exhibits to goods" has been successfully realized through bonded exhibition and sales or cross-border e-commerce mode.

Build a distinctive modern service industry cluster. Expand and deepen the platform function of Hongqiao Overseas Trade Center. As a functional platform for serving overseas non-governmental organizations, Hongqiao Overseas Trade Center has introduced five key institutions, including the International Organization for the Prevention and Resolution of Commercial Disputes, the Georgia Federation of Foreign Trade in Shanghai, the Türkiye Federation of Food and Beverage Industry Associations in Shanghai, and the Hong Kong Chinese Chamber of Commerce and Industry in Shanghai 36 international trade and investment promotion institutions, including the Hong Kong and China Chamber of Commerce and Industry, have contacted more than 150 countries and regions around the world. The new Hongqiao Overseas Trade Center sub-platform will form a service synergy with Qingpu District Commerce Commission, West Hongqiao and other departments. On November 7, the "China Imported Food Industry Summit", one of the important official supporting activities of the Import and Export Expo hosted by the China Chamber of Commerce for the Import and Export of Food, Native Produce and Animal By-products, released the "Shanghai Hongqiao · China Imported Food Trade Index" at the conference, laying a soft foundation for building the Shanghai Hongqiao Food International Trade Information Center and promoting the construction of the Shanghai Hongqiao Food

International Trade Cluster. On November 7, the Singapore China General Chamber of Commerce held the "New China Business Forum" under the theme of "New Pattern and New Opportunities" to further promote the exchange and interaction between enterprises in Singapore and China. In 2022, it will introduce 61 enterprises, serve more than 2100 overseas enterprises and carry out more than 300 economic and trade activities; We have successfully promoted the introduction of White Rabbit Milk Sugar, Sanniu Food, Yanjing Beer and other products into the markets of South Africa, Kenya and New Zealand to achieve win-win results.

We will deepen the construction of pharmaceutical clusters. In March 2010, the project was approved and launched by the executive meeting of the Shanghai Municipal Government. The whole park covers an area of 100 hectares, including 42 hectares in Phase I and 58 hectares in Phase II. In June 2017, five ministries and commissions including the National Health and Family Planning Commission selected 13 national health tourism demonstration bases across the country, and the New Hongqiao International Medical Center applied for selection on behalf of Shanghai, becoming a national health industrial park. On the plot of the first phase of the park, the Hongqiao Hospital of Huashan Hospital affiliated to Fudan University has been officially operated for four years, and the business volume has increased rapidly. Last year, more than 30000 patients were discharged, including more than 90% of patients from the Yangtze River Delta and other provinces and cities across the country. In the first phase of the park, there are also seven high-level international hospitals (social capital investment) and an intensive and shared medical technology center building (including imaging center, inspection center, drug supply center, etc.), with a total construction area of 700000 square meters, and a total investment of more than 13 billion yuan in medical industry projects.

The seven high-level international hospitals are Taihecheng Tumor Hospital, Singapore Baihui Hospital, Southwest Orthopedic Hospital, Green Leaf Medical Beauty Hospital, Xingchen Children's Hospital, Cihong Obstetrics and Gynecology Hospital, and Lanhai Rehabilitation Hospital. These hospitals cooperate with the top foreign hospitals and the city's top three hospitals through various forms of brand, technology, management and other cooperation.

Three hospitals have been approved for the second phase of the park (Green Leaf Lilan Hospital, Xiehua Brain Hospital, and Shengkangda Hospital). In addition to the hospital, the second phase introduced Xinda Biological International Operation Headquarters and Global R&D Center, Yunnan Baiyao Shanghai International Center, focusing on education, R&D, transformation and other characteristic projects in the big health industry chain.

Section Three   Focus on Building a New Platform for the International Trade Center

Accelerate the building of a new highland for trade-based headquarters. 25 supporting measures have been issued to support the recruitment of talents and talents of trade-oriented headquarters enterprises, increase financial support for trade-oriented headquarters enterprises, support trade-oriented headquarters enterprises to improve their capital operation and management capabilities, support trade-oriented headquarters to improve their trade scale, support trade-oriented headquarters enterprises to expand the international market, and improve the service mechanism of trade-oriented headquarters enterprises. The first batch of 30 trade-oriented headquarters has been identified, covering a variety of trade modes such as new cross-border e-commerce, offshore resale, bonded display, guaranteed transfer to cross-border, guaranteed transfer to exhibition, and trans-protection. There are 7 domestic wholesale and retail, 7 international goods trade, 12 international services and logistics, and 4 platform transactions, accounting for 23.3%, 23.3%, 40% and 13.4% respectively. The top 5 international trade enterprises account for nearly 23% of the import and export trade volume of the business zone.

Accelerate the construction of the headquarters cluster of private enterprises in the Yangtze River Delta. Set up a private enterprise headquarters cultivation base in Hongqiao International CBD, encourage enterprises to accelerate the business gathering and function expansion in Hongqiao International CBD, upgrade to become private enterprise headquarters, carry out integrated innovation, development and expansion in the industrial chain, value chain and innovation chain, and accelerate the building of a private enterprise headquarters cluster in the Yangtze River Delta.

The Hongqiao International CBD has gathered all kinds of high-end talents at home and abroad, especially the "concentric circle" of the Hongqiao International CBD has attracted a large number of cross-city commuting "migrant talents" in the Yangtze River

Delta. The employment scale of cross-city commuting has increased by about 47% in the past three years. At the same time, it has created a lot of investment opportunities for private enterprises. In 2022, the Hongqiao International CBD has attracted more than 80 billion yuan of key projects, involving 72 private enterprise investment projects (nearly half of which are enterprises in the Yangtze River Delta), with a total investment of 45 billion yuan, covering such industries as biomedicine, digital technology, semiconductor, new energy, etc. On this basis, the Hongqiao International CBD has identified 34 private enterprise headquarters in 2022, including many high-energy and new track leading enterprises, such as Midea Shanghai headquarters, Condolet Group, Huadian Navigation, and well-known consumer brands "Vipshop", "Rejoice Bird", "Macalline", etc.

From the perspective of enterprise investment scale, the operating income of 34 private enterprise headquarters in 2021 will exceed 50 billion yuan, and the total tax amount will reach 2.2 billion yuan, accounting for about 6% of the total tax revenue of the Hongqiao International CBD; From the perspective of enterprise industrial layout, more than 70% of enterprises are highly matched with the "four high and five new" industrial system in the Hongqiao International CBD, including the digital new economy represented by Guanglianda, Zhongying Electronics, and Huadian Navigation, the new life technology represented by Condolet and Betani, the low-carbon new energy represented by remolding technology, the new forces of automobile represented by Weima Automobile and Ritai Automobile, and the new forces of automobile represented by Midea, Bosden, Vipshop, Baoxiniao, Macalline Fashionable new consumption represented by Di Sante and the formation of a distinctive industrial ecosystem have accelerated; From the perspective of the coordinated development of the Yangtze River Delta, the industrial linkage is closer, and more than 70% of the first identified enterprises are headquarters enterprises in the Yangtze River Delta.

With its headquarters in Hongqiao and its branches and production bases in the Yangtze River Delta, the energy level has risen; Or the group authorized, managed and R&D headquarters to settle in Hongqiao, which is in line with the advantages of Shanghai. The industrial linkage development pattern of "headquarters+base" has become increasingly clear and has gradually become a new path for the development of headquarters enterprises.

Promote the global digital trading port to take the lead. Hongqiao International CBD is a key area for the development of digital trade in Shanghai. 2022 is the third year of the implementation of the Three-Year Action Plan for the Construction of the Global Digital Trade Port in Hongqiao International CBD. According to the "one hub, three centers" framework of building a digital trade hub linking the whole country and the world, building a digital trade enterprise growth center, a spillover effect transformation center for the Expo and the Yangtze River Delta digital trade promotion center, focusing on cross-border e-commerce, digital content, digital services and industrial applications and cloud services, Highlighting the gathering of digital trade service functions, the Hongqiao International CBD has gathered more than 7000 digital economy enterprises, including more than 2200 enterprises of considerable scale, and a number of leading enterprises and unicorn enterprises represented by Ctrip, iQIYI, Lianying, China Test Navigation, On-cloud Exhibition, Neusoft, EDG, RNG, etc. have emerged; A group of e-commerce social platform enterprises represented by Baiqiu, Rongmiao, Yifei, Xinyiteng, Guoquan, Yangqiaoyuan, Jinjia Technology, etc; A group of digital content and digital service enterprises represented by Zebra Zhixing, Core Yihui, Wansheng Huaxing, Xiaoi Robot, Black Lake Technology, Graffiti Intelligence, Zhenkunxing, Danaher, Dipler, Lianying, Guanglianda, and Hengshi Computer Information Technology, focus on exhibition, business, tourism, logistics, medical, education, culture, training and other industries, cultivate new models of digital trade, and develop new models of digital trade in intelligent networked automobile, industrial Internet Digital content and other fields form industrial development clusters.

Deeply promote the construction of the global digital trading port bearing platform, and add China's Beidou Industrial Technology Innovation Hongqiao Base as the first batch of national geographic information service characteristic service export bases; Hongqiao Pinhui is newly added as the first batch of Shanghai broadcast e-commerce base; The new "source of Hongqiao" online new economic ecological park, Ctrip Smart Travel Park, Unilever U Innovation Incubator, and Xingjian SPACE Incubator have accelerated their development; The National Foreign Culture and Trade Base (Shanghai) Beihongqiao Innovation Center has introduced nearly 200 digital culture and related industrial chain enterprises with an output value of more than 500 million; Hongqiao Import Commodities Exhibition and Trading Center, Shanghai Hongqiao Airport Economic Park and other municipal cross-border e-commerce demonstration zones, Shanghai Hongqiao Airport Economic Park, Shanghai West Hongqiao Business Development Co., Ltd. - West Hongqiao International CBD and other municipal service trade promotion demonstration bases, as well as Microsoft Hongqiao Digital Trade Industry Innovation and Empowerment Center and other functions have emerged. Actively support the establishment of a national digital service export base in the airport economic park, promote the implementation of the international Internet data channel, and explore a high-level cross-border data flow open system.

Implement the planning and construction of online new economic ecological park in Hongqiao International CBD. Focusing on the goal and task of taking the lead in building a global digital trading port and creating a national digital service export base, the Hongqiao International CBD actively grasps the advantages of the three core functions of "big transportation, big exhibition, and big business" closely related to the flow, grabs the development trend of digital new ecology and new business forms, actively layout and seize the digital new track, and jointly plans the construction of "Hongqiao International Online New Economic Ecological Park" with the Municipal Economic and Information Commission, Inject new momentum into regional development.

It is clearly proposed that the scale of online new economy will exceed 500 billion yuan by 2025; Introduce more than 50 leading enterprises and chain owners, 200 growth enterprises, and gather more than 3500 online new economy enterprises with innovative vitality and potential; Launch more than 50 application demonstration scenarios; Introduce 2 large courtyards and 2 joint laboratories; The development goal of basically building a triangular digital brain framework.

The online new economic and ecological park is based on the pattern of "one core and four zones" cluster and collaborative development, covering a total area of 22.92 square kilometers, with a total planned space carrier area of about 14.635 million square meters, and the space carrier area that can be put into use is about 10.998 million square meters, focusing on the six characteristic industries of digital trade, digital exhibition, digital content, digital health, industrial Internet, and digital travel, and exploring and grasping the metauniverse, quantum information Big data and aerospace information are the four leading industries. Adhere to the two-wheel drive of industrial digitalization and digital industrialization, strengthen the characteristics, break through the frontier, build the traffic convergence area of Hongqiao International Open Hub, and explore and create the value of Hongqiao traffic.

With the support of the Municipal Commission of Economic and Information Technology and the four district governments, the Management Committee took the lead in the overall planning, and actively planned and arranged 20 key projects in advance, involving six major areas : digital trade, digital content, digital health, digital travel, industrial Internet, and the metauniverse. At the "Chaochung Pujiang Investment in Hongqiao" event, the municipal leaders announced that the construction of "Hongqiao International Online New Economic Ecological Park" was started. With the care and support of the municipal party committee and the municipal government, "Hongqiao International Online New Economic Ecological Park" was included in the work task of the Shanghai 2022 Government Work Report.

Section Four   Focus on Improving the Comprehensive Traffic Management Level

Following the principles of international first-class, hub leading, open and interconnected, green and low-carbon, three-dimensional integration, integrated layout, intelligent interconnection, and overall coordination, focusing on hubs, channels, networks and management, the "1551" overall layout of the long-term comprehensive transport planning of the Hongqiao International Central Business District is proposed, which is "a hub system with one main and four auxiliary, a connection channel with five directions, a regional network with five systems, and an integrated and interconnected integrated platform".

Prepare comprehensive transportation planning. In order to promote a new round of higher quality development of the Hongqiao International Central Business District, coordinate with the "Medium and Short Term Planning of the Land Space of the Hongqiao International Central Business District", and guide the planning, construction and management of the comprehensive transportation of the Hongqiao International Central Business District, the CBD launched the preparation of the "Special Plan for the Comprehensive Transportation of the Hongqiao International Central Business District" at the beginning of 2022.

Focusing on the construction of important facilities and the key issues of improving the traffic accessibility and comprehensive management level in the core area, it clarified the objectives of the planning, construction and management of the comprehensive traffic in the Hongqiao International CBD, highlighted the development characteristics of the "international positioning, opening advantages, hub functions" of the Hongqiao International CBD, and reflected the idea of "high-quality, integrated" urban development.

Optimize the comprehensive transportation system of hubs, channels, networks and platforms. A hub system of "one main and four auxiliary" will be formed to improve the ability to radiate the region and link with the world. "One main" is the comprehensive transportation hub of Hongqiao, which strengthens the function of international and domestic gateway hub. The "four auxiliary" are four regional hubs, taking into account the intercity services in the adjacent areas of the Yangtze River Delta. Through the construction of regional hubs and anchoring of municipal railways, urban rail transit, public transport, slow traffic, etc., realize the integrated development of rail public transport slow traffic.

A five-way internal and external connection channel will be formed. Through the construction of trunk railways, the construction of municipal railways and the improvement of expressways, five radiation channels will continue to be built in the direction of the Hongqiao International CBD and the central urban area, the direction of the Pudong hub - the new port area, the north expansion belt of the Yangtze River Delta, the south expansion belt and the demonstration area. To form a regional transportation network of five systems and create international first-class CBD travel services. To form and build an integrated interconnected comprehensive traffic management system and realize the synergy and efficiency of the Hongqiao International CBD management.

Promote the preliminary research and implementation progress of infrastructure projects. Among the transportation facilities related to Hongqiao International CBD, the main railway lines such as the Shanghai-Suhu Railway and the riverside railway have been started and will be completed and opened to traffic in 2024 as planned. The Jiamin Line and its north extension, the airport connecting line, the Shanghai Demonstration Area Line, and the west extension of rail transit line 13 and line 2 were also started in July 2022, and completed by 2028 at the latest. The west extension of medium-volume bus No.71 has also been started, and it is planned to be completed and open to traffic in the first quarter of next year. The new project of Shanghai-Jiaxing Expressway - Jiamin Elevated Link Line was commenced in October 2022. The reconstruction and expansion project of Jiajin section of G15 highway (G1503 highway - Huqingping highway), the traffic function improvement project of S20 west section of the outer ring road, and the widening and reconstruction project of G50 Shanghai-Chongqing highway have been announced. In addition, the feasibility study of Shenchang Road - Jinyun First Road has been reported to the Municipal Development and Reform Commission and is in the stage of feasibility study evaluation; The feasibility study of

Shenkun Road - Jinyun Road has been approved and is planned to start at the end of the year. Continue to promote regional roads and improve the internal trunk road network in the four districts to further improve the internal and external traffic service capacity of the Hongqiao International CBD.

In addition, the Hongqiao international CBD continues to promote the construction of comprehensive transportation facilities, improve the comprehensive transportation system of the Hongqiao International CBD, and support the basic completion of the international open hub.

Section Five   Focus on Improving the Ability to Serve the Yangtze River Delta

Radiate the integrated development of the Yangtze River Delta. It has basically achieved one-hour commute with major cities in the Yangtze River Delta region. The civil aviation, high-speed rail and rail transit systems are relatively complete, forming a unique geographical advantage and providing convenient transportation services for business trade, talent flow and commodity circulation in the Yangtze River Delta region. Support the construction of Hongqiao "reception hall" in the cities of the Yangtze River Delta, such as Nanjing and Suzhou in Jiangsu Province, and Jiaxing and Huzhou in Zhejiang Province to set up commercial offices in the Hongqiao International CBD, comprehensively display and promote their respective characteristics and advantages, provide channels for enterprise talent recruitment, scientific research incubation, market promotion, and help the Hongqiao International Central Business District become the intersection hub of the flow economy in the Yangtze River Delta region.

Promote the coordinated opening of the Yangtze River Delta. Based on building a "new platform" of legal services facing the Yangtze River Delta, radiating across the country and connecting with the international community, we will build a comprehensive international central legal area integrating public legal services, professional legal services, legal research and exchange. Support local enterprises to expand the "the Belt and Road" national market, promote factor link, capacity link, market link, rule link, create a comprehensive service platform integrating information, financing, talent, law and risk prevention, deepen the internal opening by expanding the opening up, and accelerate the creation of a central node of the domestic big cycle and a strategic link of domestic and international double cycles.

We will promote coordinated reform in the Yangtze River Delta. The policies such as the establishment of the trademark acceptance window for enterprises in the Yangtze River Delta, the pilot of international talent management reform, and the establishment of cross-regional social organizations specified in the Overall Plan have all been implemented and have been oriented to the cross-provincial acceptance services in the Yangtze River Delta. Build Hongqiao International Service Providers Alliance, set up Hongqiao Enterprise Service Center, provide trademark registration and foreigner work permit acceptance services for enterprises in the Yangtze River Delta, handle 35 matters such as establishment and change for enterprises through the cross-provincial government service platform, and self-service terminals cover 39 counties and cities in the Yangtze River Delta.

Collaborative innovation in the Yangtze River Delta. We will strengthen the construction of the "6+365" main platform, further give full play to the functions of the two major functional platforms of the Hongqiao Import Commodities Exhibition and Trade Center and the Greenland Global Commodity Trade Port, organize and promote the settlement of the Hongqiao Import Commodities Exhibition and Trade Center in Hangzhou, Hefei, Changzhou, Huangshan, Jiaxing and other places, and gradually improve the bonded display and other functions of the import and export commodity distribution center. Relying on the Hongqiao-Kunshan-Xiangcheng comprehensive functional corridor, the Hongqiao International CBD and Kunshan strengthen the linkage of the import trade promotion and innovation demonstration zone. Promote the sharing of medical resources and technology in the New Hongqiao International Medical Center, and is becoming a "super hospital" in the Yangtze River Delta.

Strengthen the exchange and interaction between "one core" and "two belts" and cities in the Yangtze River Delta, sign strategic cooperation agreements with 24 cities in the Yangtze River Delta, promote the synergy between the Hongqiao International CBD and the Yangtze River Delta, improve the upstream and downstream industrial chain, and promote the construction of "headquarters+base" industrial clusters. Organize the promotion and project signing conference of the headquarters of private enterprises in the Yangtze River Delta, jointly with the four districts to promote investment in the Yangtze River Delta region, and successively hold the Yangtze River Delta Entrepreneur Roundtable in Hefei, Hangzhou and other places to gradually shape the investment atmosphere of the enterprises in the Yangtze River Delta to the Hongqiao International CBD, and achieve coordinated development and win-win cooperation.

The construction site meeting of Hongqiao International Open Hub was successfully held. In conjunction with the Municipal Development and Reform Commission and relevant districts, set up special classes to focus on core functions, characteristic industries and key enterprises, carefully design and arrange "enterprise exhibition center", build "enterprise service hall" and "talent port exhibition hall" with high standards, and launch a high-level "on-site exhibition point" to display artificial intelligence, digital health, digital creativity The four major industrial ecosystems, including digital travel, highlight the new momentum of the overall digital economic development of the Hongqiao International CBD, and stereoscopically present the outstanding achievements of the Hongqiao International CBD in the implementation of the national strategy of Hongqiao International Open Hub for one week. At the same time, focusing on the key areas of concern of the conference, we will carry out in-depth research work related to the Hongqiao Policy Version 2.0 of the Overall Plan, and will promote the relevant national departments to introduce a number of policies and measures with high content and strong innovation at the "Second Anniversary" on-site meeting.

Chapter III　Great Shanghai Epidemic Prevention Action

Section One　Epidemic Prevention Action

Taking epidemic prevention and control as the top political task, and under the strong leadership of the municipal party committee and the municipal government, actively working with the municipal transportation committee, Minhang District and the hub operation management unit to carry out the epidemic prevention and control work of the hub, keep the safety bottom line, and ensure the smooth operation of the Hongqiao high-speed railway station. At the same time, the backbone force was transferred to fully support the municipal emergency special needs support, the construction and operation of the municipal shelter hospital and other work, which reflected the role of the management committee in winning the "Great Shanghai Epidemic Prevention Action".

Hold the bottom line of safe operation of Hongqiao hub and the red line of epidemic prevention in the Hongqiao international CBD. Since this round of epidemic, municipal leaders have attached great importance to the operation of Hongqiao transportation hub and epidemic prevention and control. The then Secretary Li Qiang gave instructions twice, Mayor Gong Zheng went to Hongqiao Station to inspect and put forward requirements, and other city leaders successively went to the hub to inspect and guide the operation order and the work of sending students to the station. Focusing on the goal of "releasing overflows and preventing imports", the Management Committee, together with the Municipal Transportation Committee, Minhang District Government, railway, public security and other relevant units, set up special work teams to continue to carry out traffic organization, epidemic prevention and control, detention security and other work. First, organize the stranded personnel to carry out nucleic acid and antigen detection; The second is to strictly separate the moving lines for passengers to enter and exit, and carry out daily site clearing disinfection and sterilization on the arrival floor; Third, carry out remote inspection on the vehicles and personnel entering the station, and passengers who meet the conditions for leaving Shanghai and hold the tickets of the day are allowed to get off; The fourth is to distribute food, water and other basic living materials for the detained people and set up temporary settlement; Fifth, patrol the stations, streets, green belts, elevated roads and other places every day; Sixthly, the stranded passengers were classified and evacuated in an orderly manner, and the bottom line for the smooth operation of the Hongqiao hub was firmly built, which maintained the order of the hub and its surrounding areas, and contributed to ensuring the epidemic prevention and operation safety of the hub. More than 20,000 people were resettled in May. It has built a canopy of more than 2,000 square meters for the stranded people, set up 16 mobile toilets and multiple snack mobile phone charging facilities, and distributed materials daily, making positive contributions to winning the "Great Shanghai Epidemic Prevention Action".

Give full support to the coordination of emergency needs of special groups. Cooperate with relevant enterprises and local governments to build an online and offline linkage and docking platform for the "special emergency needs coordination group for special groups". Through the special channels of "emergency special needs" such as Eleme and Meituan, we can solve the urgent problems of the supply of living materials and drugs for the elderly, the weak, the sick, the disabled, the pregnant and other special groups in a timely manner. More than 440,000 emergency special work orders have been received in total, including more than 280,000 emergency special work orders for special groups, and more than 240,000 have been solved in total, with a resolution rate of more than 87%.

Fully support the construction and operation of the municipal shelter. There are nearly 50,000 beds in the square cabin of the International Exhibition Center, and about 8,000 people are transferred daily during peak hours. The pressure is great, and there is no room for loss. The special team of the management committee is responsible for the discharge and transfer of the square cabin hospital of the International Exhibition Center, and three comrades have been fighting for more than 50 days, day and night on the front line. The whole process of wall map operation, pre-arrangement scheme and optimization process have increased from about 1000 people out of the cabin every day at the beginning to more than 2000 people out of the cabin every hour, and the speed has increased by more than 10 times; Shorten the time for citizens to transfer to district and county vehicles in the parking lot, and ensure that more than 90% of the people get off immediately. At the same time, for special groups such as the young children in the shelter, a working mechanism is formed, which is taken care of by a special person, and the children are tracked to return home safely throughout the process.

Chapter IV   The Fifth China International Import Expo

Section One   Basic Overview

The fifth China International Import Expo is the first major international exhibition held in China after the 20th CPC National Congress.

On the evening of November 4, at the opening ceremony of the 5th China International Import Expo, President Xi affirmed the important role and fruitful results of the Expo in his video speech, explained the opening measures to provide new opportunities to the world with China's new development, stressed that China will promote all countries to share the three opportunities of China's big market, institutional opening and deepening international cooperation, and demonstrated China's firm determination to share development opportunities with the world, He points out the direction for the "better and better" of the Expo. Li Qiang, member of the Standing Committee of the Political Bureau of the CPC Central Committee, attended the opening ceremony and delivered a speech in Shanghai. Vice Premier Hu Chunhua and Shanghai Municipal Party Secretary Chen Jining attended the ceremony.

In the morning of November 5, the high-level forum "RCEP and a higher level of openness" was held. Vice Premier Hu Chunhua and Secretary of the Shanghai Municipal Party Committee Chen Jining attended and delivered speeches. In six days, the idea of open cooperation collided at the Hongqiao International Economic Forum, and the world's leading technical concepts were unveiled at the exhibition. Enterprises from all countries shared new opportunities for entering the Expo and the open market. The fifth China International Import Expo achieved the expected goals of safety, excellence and effectiveness.

A total of 145 countries, regions and international organizations participated in the Expo. 24 Hongqiao Forum activities were successfully held. More than 2800 enterprises from 127 countries and regions participated in the business exhibition; Showing 438 representative new products, new technologies and new services for the first time, exceeding the previous expo. The digital access platform built for the first time attracted 368 technical equipment enterprises to participate online, and organized 64 live or broadcast activities, with 600,000 views. Adhere to the development direction of "government+market", established 39 trading groups and nearly 600 trading sub-groups, 4 industrial trading groups and nearly 100 industrial trading sub-groups added. 69 countries and international organizations were on the bright line of national exhibitions, on increase of 13% over the previous session. The comprehensive exhibition area of "China's Ten Years - Opening Achievements Exhibition" shows the brilliant achievements of China's opening up in the new era in an all-round and three-dimensional way. The Expo Cultural Exhibition Center has a panoramic view of the development process and holding results of the Expo in the past five years. Professional supporting activities and people-to-people and cultural exchange activities are rich and colorful. On-site service guarantee has been continuously optimized and improved to do a good job in epidemic prevention and control. As of 12：00 on November 10, 461000 people have entered the site. The intended turnover of the Expo is 73.52 billion US dollars per year, an increase of 3.9% over the previous one. With the joint efforts of all parties, the fifth China International Import Expo has achieved the expected goals of success, excellence and effectiveness.

The opening ceremony has attracted wide attention at home and abroad. In the video address at the opening ceremony, President Xi Jinping pointed out that China will adhere to the basic national policy of opening to the outside world, adhere to the win-win strategy of opening up, adhere to the correct direction of economic globalization, promote all countries to share the opportunities of China's big market, share the opportunities of systematic opening up, and share the opportunities of deepening international cooperation, and inject strong and positive energy into creating a better future of opening up and prosperity. Li Qiang, member of the Standing Committee of the Political Bureau of the CPC Central Committee, delivered a speech at the venue, toured the enterprise exhibition before the opening ceremony, and took a group photo with the heads of key exhibitors. Leaders of many countries and heads of international organizations made speeches in video. Vice Premier Hu Chunhua presided over the opening ceremony. 101 above ministerial level guests from 82 countries, regions and international organizations attended online.

The Hongqiao Forum gathers open consensus. In terms of key activities, the "RCEP and a higher level of openness" high-level forum invited guests from all walks of life in politics, business, science and research to participate in the discussion on the important topics such as the RCEP agreement that came into force in 2022, regional economic integration and a higher level of openness, and contributed wisdom to the construction of an open world economy. The release of the World Open Report 2022 and the international seminar released the latest World Open Index, deeply explored the rules of opening up, and made efforts to build a "weathervane" and "barometer" in the field of world opening up. In terms of speakers, a total of 385 guests delivered online and offline speeches or participated in the discussion during the 24 events, including 9 political dignitaries at or above the vice national level, 68 political dignitaries at or above the provincial and ministerial level, 3 Nobel Prize winners, 19 academicians of the Chinese Academy of Sciences and Chinese Academy of Social Sciences, and other well-known experts and scholars, as well as executives of the world's top 500 and industry leading enterprises. In terms of the participation of professional institutions, 9 central ministries and commissions, 4 local provinces and cities, and 3 professional think tanks jointly hosted the sub-forums of professional fields; During the period, 17 professional reports were released to build the "flagship report of the World Open Report 2022"+"brand report of professional fields"+"professional report of sub-forum co-sponsors" result system. In terms of participation of international organizations, six new international organizations, including the United Nations Industrial Development Organization, the United Nations Population Fund, the United Nations Global Compact, the United Nations Office for Disaster Reduction, the International Trade Centre and the World Intellectual Property Organization, have been added to host sub-forums to invite more international guests to participate.

The quality of enterprise business exhibition is better. A total of 284 of the world's top 500 and industry leading enterprises participated in the exhibition. The number exceeded that of the previous session. The return rate was nearly 90%. The proportion of special booth decoration reached 96.1%, which was higher than that of the previous session. The food and agricultural products exhibition area has the largest number of participating countries and enterprises, with 1076 enterprises from 104 countries participating. The auto exhibition area highlighted intelligent low carbon and displays the latest development achievements of the global auto industry. The technology and equipment exhibition area focused on "double carbon", integrated circuit, artificial intelligence and other hot areas, and focuses on displaying cutting-edge technologies and high-end equipment. The consumer goods exhibition area released many first-issue exhibits, actively advocating a green and sustainable lifestyle. The exhibition area of medical devices and medical care attracted the world's top 15 drug giants and top 10 medical device enterprises to participate in the exhibition, and the public health epidemic prevention zone intensively displayed the international advanced public health epidemic prevention achievements. The service trade exhibition area gathered 39 of the world's top 500 and industry leading enterprises, as well as the hidden champions in many segments. In the innovation incubation zone, 153 small and micro-enterprises of scientific and technological innovation displayed innovative products in a centralized manner, and the selection activity attracted the attention of a large number of netizens.

The National Comprehensive Exhibition created an immersive viewing experience. As an important part of the Expo, the National Exhibition has always adhered to the global public goods attribute, constantly innovated the exhibition display methods, and attracted the wide participation of all countries in the world. This online national exhibition has a total of 69 countries and international organizations appearing in the newly created digital exhibition hall. With the help of immersive display, all exhibitors have fully displayed their wonderful contents in the fields of scientific and technological innovation, culture and art, investment environment, etc., with a total of 59 million visits, more than the previous one. The head of Monaco, as well as ministerial officials from Austria, Nepal, Costa Rica, Iceland, the United Arab Emirates, Italy and other countries, ambassadors to China and heads of trade promotion agencies, addressed the national exhibition through video, and highly recognized the role of the Fair in promoting the sharing of development opportunities among all countries.

Improve the quality and efficiency of professional supporting activities. Central ministries and commissions, local governments and international organizations held 98 supporting on-site activities, covering policy interpretation, docking and signing, product display, investment promotion, research and release, and the quality and effectiveness of the activities were further improved. The trade and investment matchmaking meeting between China and the exhibition has reached 293 cooperation intentions, with the total amount of intention to sign more than US $5.9 billion. Organized 82 centralized signing activities and reached more than 600 intentional cooperation. Organized special online matchmaking activities to promote exhibitors and buyers to carry out cloud communication and negotiate contracts. 94 new product launches were held and 171 cutting-edge scientific and technological products were displayed.

The people-to-people and cultural exchange activities are rich and colorful. The total exhibition area of people-to-people and cultural exchange activities has increased to 32,000 square meters, which is the largest in the past. Italy, the Hong Kong Special Administrative Region and 30 provinces and municipalities organized 715 institutions participated in the exhibition, and the number of exhibitors increased by 16% compared with the previous session. 239 intangible cultural heritage projects, 275 time-honored brands and 10 national demonstration pedestrian streets displayed their distinctive contents. To build a "cultural block", 10 provinces, regions and cities have set up long-term exhibition halls for cultural exchanges, with a total area of more than 12000 square meters. A number of art performance groups presented 54 high-level cultural public welfare performances, including 4 world-class intangible cultural heritage projects and 9 national intangible cultural heritage projects, with a total of 75 performances. For the first time, art groups from Hong Kong, China, have stepped on the stage.

Practical and effective on-site service of the exhibition. The function of "ordering food online and picking up food at the store" was optimized, dining seats added, and the risk of crowd gathering was reduced. The world's first multi-type intelligent robot cluster service was introduced to create a virtual and real interactive experience for the exhibition visitors. We also further strengthened technology empowerment and provided accurate, convenient and non-invasive intelligent epidemic prevention support for participants. We strengthened the mobile terminal guidance service function, and realized the positioning and navigation in the library and the access of information at any time. Design and develop cultural and creative products such as cultural and creative products for the fifth anniversary of the Expo, Expo professional series blind box, and the art derivatives of the Expo to show the charm of the Expo culture and art. Adhere to the "green, environmental protection and sustainable" exhibition orientation, promote the "carbon neutral" project, introduce the carbon inclusive mechanism, and create the "zero carbon into the Expo".

Section Four   Basic Overview of the Hongqiao HUB Conference

In the morning of November 6, 2022, the fifth Hongqiao International Economic Forum "Hongqiao International Open Hub Construction Forum and 2022 Hongqiao HUB Conference", co-sponsored by the Shanghai Municipal People's Government, the National Development and Reform Commission and the Ministry of Commerce, was held in the 4.2 Hall of the National Convention and Exhibition Center (Shanghai). The report of the 20th National Congress of the Communist Party of China pointed out that the door of China's opening will only be wider and wider. In the video speech at the opening ceremony of the 5th China International Import Expo, the General Secretary pointed out that openness is an important driving force for the progress of human civilization and the only way for the prosperity and development of the world. The theme of this Hongqiao HUB Conference is "Hongtu Exhibition · Bridging the World – Open and Enjoy the Future", "Look at the hub with opening, and the hub is in Hongqiao" as the main line, and the focus is on the hub in opening, the hub in strategy, and the hub in development. It shows the era opportunity of high-level opening, the era requirements of high-quality development, highlights the main theme of opening, and the new value of the hub.

The forum focused on better building a new development pattern, deeply implemented the national strategy of integrated development of the Yangtze River Delta, gathered the insights of guests from all walks of life in politics, business, education and research, profoundly interpreted the open and sharing attitude of Hongqiao, fully explored the core functions of Hongqiao International Open Hub, and vividly displayed the construction results of Hongqiao International Open Hub. The forum, in resonance with Expo, outlined a panoramic picture of the opening and construction of Hongqiao International Open Hub. The agenda of the conference always runs through the two major themes of the era of "high level" and "high quality", closely links the two sectors at home and abroad, organically integrates the cross-border wisdom of academia and industry, and builds a two-way link fast lane with the "rainbow bridge". The world's top scholars and industry leaders carried out concentrated discussions on the construction of the two-way hub under the new pattern, and made suggestions for the high-quality development of the Hongqiao International Open Hub under the new pattern of global opening through the international environment, regional opening, cooperation situation and other perspectives, sending out the "Hongqiao voice" of opening and sharing to the world, and constantly promoting regional collaborative innovation and development.

In the preparation stage of the forum, under the guidance and support of the Municipal Commission of Commerce, the Municipal Development and Reform Commission, the Import Expo Bureau and other institutions, the Management Committee made the preparation of the forum a top priority, fully coordinated the resources of all parties, and fully promoted the planning and preparation of the forum. On the one hand, it pays attention to the program planning to highlight the "Hongqiao wisdom". The Management Committee fully mobilized its internal research force and external intellectual support, focused on exploring and highlighting the core functions of the Hongqiao hub, confirmed the overall consideration of the forum, brand building, sponsor, time and place and scope of attendance as soon as possible, finalized the key guests for sharing with various resources, and organized the writing of the core materials of the forum speech to assist relevant guests and media in digging the development code of Hongqiao, laying a solid foundation for the smooth holding of the forum. On the other hand, focus on implementation to highlight "Hongqiao efficiency". The Management Committee cooperated and organized relevant departments and units to form five working groups, including "comprehensive coordination, conference services, logistics support, reception and liaison, and news publicity", and organized thematic meetings for many times to coordinate and promote the implementation of the "one guest one team" reception plan according to the division of labor, and ensured that the forum is held and guests are received without any loss.

At the opening ceremony, Gong Zheng, Deputy Secretary of the Shanghai Municipal Party Committee and Mayor, Wang Shouwen, Deputy Secretary of the Party Leadership Group of the Ministry of Commerce, International Trade Negotiator and Deputy Minister,

Guo Lanfeng, Member of the Party Leadership Group of the National Development and Reform Commission, and Wang Zhiheng, Vice President of the Bank of China delivered the opening speech. Zong Ming, Deputy Mayor of Shanghai and Director of the Management Committee of Hongqiao International Central Business District, presided over the opening ceremony.

In the keynote speech, Mark, President of the New Development Bank, and Thomas Sargent, winner of the Nobel Prize in Economics, delivered keynote speeches, emphasizing the importance of openness from an economic point of view, and providing suggestions for the construction of the new platform of the International Central Business District and the International Trade Center. Han Weiwen, president of Bain Corporation in China and member of the global board of directors, Wang Yiming, deputy chairman of the China Center for International Economic Exchanges, Liu Shijin, deputy director of the Economic Committee of the National Committee of the Chinese People's Political Consultative Conference, Zhou Kui, partner of Sequoia China, Luo Kangrui, chairman of Ruian Group, and many other top scholars and industry leaders from around the world delivered keynote speeches, sharing insights from all aspects and perspectives, and promoting Hongqiao to continuously explore and improve its service to the national unified market The Yangtze River Economic Belt and the Yangtze River Delta have integrated construction capacity, improved the construction of the "four high and five new" industrial system, strengthened the building of talent flow hubs, trade flow hubs, digital flow hubs, capital flow hubs, and continued to gather key elements such as passenger flow, logistics, capital flow, and information flow, and made every effort to promote the industrial linkage, enterprise interaction, and resource flow in the Yangtze River Delta, and constantly create a new situation of regional coordinated development.

During the round-table discussion, a group of representative experts or entrepreneurs, including Wei Zhe, chairman and founding partner of Jiayu Capital, Cui Zhihui, executive director and chief executive officer of Manpower China, Ye Fei, president and chief executive officer of Michelin China, Liu Zhicheng, chairman and CEO of Buy Quickly Group, and Yang Mingchao, founder and chairman of Guoquan, had a round-table dialogue to deeply explore the core functions of Hongqiao International Open Hub, Insights into the trend of regional coordinated development, interprets the opportunities of international coordinated opening, and excavates the endogenous power of regional economy.

At the publicity stage of the forum, the management committee paid attention to elaborately planning a series of publicity reports. In the pre-warm-up stage, advertisement with the theme of the HUB conference in the core area of the Hongqiao international CBD is more than two thirds. With the theme release, theme interpretation, promotional film broadcast, key interviews, and public promotion and dissemination, the brand of "Hongqiao HUB Conference" is interpreted around the theme, reflecting the internationalization, openness, and pivot of the Hongqiao International Central Business District, arousing attention and expectation. During the conference, efforts were made to expand the dissemination and influence of "Hongqiao HUB Conference" through comprehensive, multi-angle and three-dimensional centralized publicity and reporting. The live broadcast volume of the conference reached tens of thousands, and the Internet communication capacity of the forum was expanded simultaneously. During the extended reporting period after the conference, the impact of follow-up reports such as the refining of conference results, the playback of highlights, and the in-depth processing of content continued to expand. Central and local media such as the People's Daily, Xinhua News Agency, Guangming Daily, Jiefang Daily, and First Financial launched a series of text and video reports, and authoritative programs such as News Network and News of the World were mainly broadcast, triggering hundreds of millions of reading and broadcasting.

The conference guests agreed that the Hongqiao International CBD has made remarkable achievements. As the "one core" in the "one core, two belts", the Hongqiao International Central Business District, closely followed the two key words of "integration" and "high quality", has made every effort to promote the implementation of the "Overall Plan for the Construction of Hongqiao International Open Hub" in the struggle of "secondary development" and "secondary entrepreneurship", and the regional economic development has run out of "acceleration" : the tax revenue in 2021 increased by 29.1% over the previous year, 11.7 percentage points faster than the average growth rate of Shanghai. From January to September 2022, after deducting the tax deduction and refund factors, the tax revenue was 29.363 billion yuan, up 3.0% year on year, the actual amount of foreign investment increased by 165.7% year on year, and the total amount of import and export commodities increased by 31.9% year on year. In 2022, it attracted nearly 130 billion yuan of key investment, an increase of more than 60% over last year. In 2022, Hongqiao International Central Business District attracted more than 500 headquarters enterprises, including 44 headquarters enterprises of multinational companies, 44 headquarters of private enterprises, 33 trade headquarters and 11 research and development centers recognized by the municipal level; There are more than 5000 international trade enterprises and 35 global trade and investment promotion institutions. The "Rainbow Bridge" connecting the international and domestic markets is speeding up its formation, becoming a high-profile new benchmark for high-speed development and a new landmark for two-way opening in the Yangtze River Delta region.

The conference guests unanimously said that the Hongqiao International CBD, as the core bearing area of the international opening hub, has the potential for continuous upgrading. Give full play to the portal function of Hongqiao transportation hub, accelerate the construction of cross-regional rail transit network, improve the air-rail intermodal transport mode, and promote the flow of resource elements and regional coordinated development. The development form of the hub has evolved from a transportation hub to a resource element hub, the development mode has changed from a single function to a multi-function integration, the core function has changed from goods distribution to an intelligent network platform, and the radiation space has expanded from the surrounding area to a larger spatial scale. The hub enables economic factors to gather more closely, minimizing the costs of labor, manufacturing, research and development, and improving efficiency, including logistics efficiency and shopping convenience, by shortening the distance, so as to enjoy the benefits of increasing returns to scale. Hongqiao International Central Business District has a good strategic position, which will become a powerful boost for the establishment of a new model of "space economy" in the Yangtze River Delta, and has the potential to become a world-class smart infrastructure hub, making contributions to China's modernization and global sustainable development.

The guests at the conference all expected that the Hongqiao International Central Business District will achieve greater development in the future. Focusing on the "3+6" leading industry in Shanghai and the requirement of developing the "five oriented economy", the "Hongqiao International Central Business District Industrial Development Plan" has recently been prepared and released, and it is proposed that by 2025, efforts should be made to build the "four high and five new" industrial system, and regular rolling improvement and adjustment should be made; We will lay out and build four 100-billion-level industrial ecological clusters of "high-flow trade economy, high-end service economy, digital new economy, and fashion new consumption", and cultivate and develop three 50-billion-level industrial clusters of "new life technology, new automobile power, and low-carbon new energy". "The target vision of Hongqiao International Central Business District is to increase the gross domestic product from 140 billion yuan to 600 billion yuan by 2035; increase the tax revenue from 34.6 billion yuan to 150 billion yuan, and strive to reach 200 billion yuan; and gather more than 1500 headquarters of all kinds." The development prospect of the Hongqiao international CBD will be brighter.

Chapter V   Coordinated Development of Four Regions

Section Four   Jiading Region

In 2022, Jiading put forward the action plan of "doubling in three years" and "doubling in five years" for the Beihongqiao International Central Business District (that is, by 2023, the tax revenue will increase by 100% compared with 2020; by 2025, the tax revenue will increase by 200% compared with 2020). Under the strong leadership of the district party committee and the district government, Beihongqiao Business District plays a strategic engine role, optimizes various mechanisms, solves various problems, and vigorously promotes the work. In order to better carry out the work, at the beginning of the year, Jiading District formulated the Action Plan for the Implementation of Secretary Li Qiang's Important Speech on the Investigation and Research of Hongqiao International Central Business District, which subdivided 44 key tasks into months, and made full efforts to promote the project construction, industrial development, policy implementation and other aspects of work, so as to ensure the implementation of all work.

By the end of October, the accumulated tax revenue was 3.557 billion yuan, 61.52% of the annual plan; The accumulated solid investment was 4.92 billion yuan, 59.13% of the annual task; The total output of key industries reached 7.52 billion yuan, 90.93% of the annual plan; 6562 enterprises have been added in total, accounting for 65.62% of the annual plan; A total of 64 new projects worth 100 million yuan have been introduced, accounting for 128% of the annual plan; Totally 16 new headquarters projects have been introduced, accounting for 160% of the annual plan; There are 4 new land acquisition and 2 new construction projects in the "four batches" industry.

By the end of October, the accumulative investment of key government investment projects had reached 129 million yuan, 48% of the annual target; The accumulative investment of major projects reached 2.44 billion yuan, 77% of the annual target. Four pieces of land were transferred.

Judging from the trend of economic indicators, the initial stage was good, with tax revenue of 1.551 billion yuan in January-February, up 29.2% year on year; The fixed investment was 1.166 billion yuan, up 101.7% year on year. During the epidemic from March to May, the progress and investment of some projects were affected to some extent. Through concerted efforts and implementation, the economic situation from June to December showed a trend of stabilization and improvement. In September, 1676 new households were added in a single month, with an annual cumulative increase of 80.56% year on year. The total number of projects introduced with 100 million yuan ranked first in the region. The number of new headquarters projects exceeded the annual target. The total output of the industry grew rapidly, especially the output of precision medicine, which reached a monthly output of 430 million yuan in October, with a completion rate of 126.47%. In the fourth quarter of the year, we will maintain the momentum of decisive victory, strengthen the promotion of our work, reverse the time nodes against the annual goals, strengthen supervision and supervision, and promote our efforts to achieve the annual goals.

The construction of key regions continued to improve quality and efficiency. The three benchmark projects of "one district, one city and one bay" have achieved new results. In the urban renewal area of Beihongqiao, the relocation of the initial plot is nearing the end. The signing rate between enterprises and farmers has reached 99%. A total of 497 farmers have signed contracts and 123 enterprises have signed contracts, striving to realize the transfer of plots within the year; The government and enterprises have basically reached a consensus on the regional general plan, and have established a working mechanism for the joint investment promotion of government and enterprises, and formed a work plan. Lingang Jiading Science and Technology City, the first project "Beihong Cloud" will start the superstructure construction within the year; The preliminary plan was formed for the preliminary work of the "village in the city" project; The second phase of the project has completed the conceptual design and is actively docking with the preliminary work of land transfer. Hongqiao Xinhui Headquarter Bay, the first phase of which has transferred 8 plots to achieve full construction; Kelly and Aohai projects have been announced on the standard land, and the land transfer will be completed in the near future; Fulong and Yifei land use projects are fully promoting land transfer. At the same time, it has reserved 13 high-quality enterprise headquarters projects such as Asia, Kaiying Network and Donghao Lansheng, and its development potential continues to increase.

The construction of key projects was comprehensively and orderly promoted. The Beihongqiao Business District is benchmarking the annual targets and tasks, focusing on the progress of the "four batches" major industrial projects with the action plan and the overall control plan as the starting point. Weilai International Headquarters Project is about to complete the planning adjustment and approval work; Tianruijin and Kangdelai consumables projects have been started; The Huazhu headquarters project is about to be completed; The comprehensive completion acceptance of Aokangda second-hand car exhibition and trading center project is about to be completed; The construction of Jiangsu Guotai Center and Kangdelai Medical Device Base has been steadily promoted.

Investment promotion and investment attraction are constantly gaining momentum. It has continuously docked with more than 10 platform institutions such as KPMG China, China Chamber of Commerce for the Import and Export of Food, Soil and Livestock, Türkiye Food Association, further strengthened the docking with Hongqiao resources, and also established a joint investment promotion mechanism with Beihong Real Estate and Jiading Science and Technology City in Lingang, playing a combination of industrial chain investment promotion, policy investment promotion, and capital investment promotion. By carrying out various activities such as "cloud investment promotion", "cloud contract signing" and "cloud negotiation", we will comprehensively promote investment promotion to a new level. In 2022, 16 projects have been signed and to be signed, with a total investment of 6.4 billion yuan. At present, we are in in-depth discussions with American Auto Bridge, Wanyang Group, Meide Medical and other projects, and continue to create a hot investment attraction situation of integration of blocks, rolling plates, and flowering at multiple points. Take advantage of the opportunity of the Yangtze River Delta Entrepreneur Roundtable and other activities to carry out the "going out" publicity work, hold the "Hongqiao flag" high, play the "Hongqiao brand" well, and continue to follow up through the establishment of special classes for major projects, so as to achieve rapid response, synergy and efficiency, and attract high-quality enterprises to land. In addition, we have completed the layout of Beihongqiao regional space resource carriers, produced a new version of Beihongqiao promotional film, brochures, policy foldouts and industrial resource maps, and further enriched the investment promotion tools.

The urban supporting construction continued to improve. The construction of traffic road network has been strengthened. The construction of Jinyuan Fifth Road Station and Jinyun Road Station of Jiamin Rail Transit Line was started, and the west extension plan of Line 14 was formed in the middle term of the study; The two district roads, Jinyun Road - Shenkun Road and Jinyuan First Road - Shenchang Road, have obtained the approval of the project construction document and are promoting the relevant work in the early stage of the project commencement; Huajiang Road Bridge, Jihe Road Bridge and Lintao Road Bridge across Wusong River were completed and opened to traffic smoothly.

The urban infrastructure has been continuously optimized. Implement the rainwater pipe renovation project of Jinyuan 4th Road and Jinyuan 8th Road to alleviate the problem of water accumulation in the flood season of Jinbao Park; Accelerate the reconstruction of Shahe Road and Xinghua Road, complete the construction of some sections of Kuangxiang Road, and continue to break through the traffic congestion points in the town; Yangliuqiao, Huiping Road, Wujiating and other resettlement bases have been fully resumed, and the construction has been carried out in an orderly manner.

The quality of public services has been continuously improved. The allocation of educational resources continued to be optimized, and the internal upgrading and optimization of Hefang Kindergarten and Jinhe Primary School Gymnasium were completed; Yangliu Middle School added a primary school department to cooperate with the Second Middle School in Jiading District; The construction of a close medical union was accelerated, and the Longhu Community Health Service Station was completed and delivered.

Chapter VI   Create a High–Quality Business Environment

Section Two   Construction of Talent Highland

The Business District has actively reported and communicated with the relevant municipal departments, issued a distinctive talent highland construction plan for the Business District, continued to build the professional brand of Hongqiao International Business Talent Port, built a first-class service platform for regional talent cooperation and exchange and convenient handling, and made future plans on the relevant measures of high-level talent introduction, international talent introduction and excellent young talent introduction, Continuously improve the core competitiveness of talent service in Hongqiao International CBD, and promote the business environment of Hongqiao International CBD with talent service. In September 2021, China's Shanghai Human Resources Industrial Park Hongqiao Park was officially approved by the Ministry of Human Resources and Social Security. On February 14, 2022, as the core carrier of the physical operation of Hongqiao International Business Talent Port, the enterprise service center of Hongqiao International Central Business District was put into trial operation; On February 25, Hongqiao Park, Shanghai Human Resources Industrial Park, China, officially opened.

First, promote the construction of talent platform. Together with Minhang District, the exhibition hall of Hongqiao International Business Talent Port will be established in the core area of Hongqiao International CBD. The government service function of talents will be incorporated into the business service center of the CBD. A comprehensive service window will be set up to provide services such as talent introduction, residence permit points, overseas student settlement, foreign talents' residence in China and work permit. Relying on the one-stop service center of Hongqiao Overseas Talents in East Hongqiao District and Changning District, the Hongqiao International Business Talents Port Changning Sub-center will be established to handle the employment, entry and exit certificates, foreign expert certificates, overseas talent residence certificates (commonly known as "B cards") and other matters for foreigners, Taiwan, Hong Kong and Macao personnel.

The second is to promote the construction of immigration policy practice base. The Administrative Measures for the Recognition of Foreign High-level Talents Recommended by the Business District to Apply for Permanent Residence in China (for Trial Implementation) (hereinafter referred to as the Administrative Measures) was formulated, filed with the National Immigration Administration, and the implementation of the operation was promoted. In August 2022, the first enterprise has completed the recommendation of permanent residence of foreign high-level talents. With the support and guidance of the municipal public security entry-exit management department, together with the Minhang District Administrative Service Center, the public security department and the South Hongqiao Company, the construction of the foreigner service window in the business district enterprise service center has been promoted. Since its operation, more than 1300 businesses have been handled by the end of September. The special service business of international school visa processing window was opened to solve the problems of visa expiration and the backlog of international school visa business caused by the closure and control of the epidemic, and help the international schools in the jurisdiction to resume work and school as soon as possible. 201 foreign teachers and staff and their families from 9 international schools have already handled the business. At the same time, in accordance with the relevant requirements of immigration integration services, and in cooperation with the entry and exit departments of Minhang District, the "Hongqiao Business District Immigration Integration Service Station" will be built to provide policy advice for foreigners working in the business district and help enterprises solve the practical problems encountered by foreign talents.

The third is to promote the safe housing of talents. Promote the acceptance and rent allocation of talent housing in the business district. Housing resources of talent housing：Xuhui talent apartment has a total construction area of 6136.24 square meters, with 112 housing resources; Le Xianju talent apartment has a total floor area of 84049.84 m^2 and a total of 1561 apartments. As of October 2022, 16 batches of applications for safe housing have been accepted. Xuhui has rented 119 apartments and Le Xianju has rented 1327 apartments. At the same time, actively connect with the market rental housing, arrange the demand of housing and white-collar workers, build a supply and demand connection platform, and serve the white-collar workers to live in peace.

Fourth, promote the construction of the Human Resources Industrial Park in Shanghai, China. The Hongqiao Industrial Park takes the space of about 17000 square meters in Building 4, 2377 Shenkun Road, as the main building of the Hongqiao Industrial Park, attracting human resources enterprises, focusing on introducing industry leading enterprises and platform resource-based enterprises, and gradually forming a large-scale industrial park. By October 2022, 95 professional institutions have settled in the park, including Ingmar Group, Social Security Technology, Shanghai Foreign Service, Huanchuang Group, Zhongyun Group, Xinhua Human Resources Group and other high-quality enterprises.

图书在版编目(CIP)数据

2022上海虹桥国际中央商务区发展报告 / 上海虹桥国际中央商务区管理委员会编 .— 上海 ：上海社会科学院出版社，2023
ISBN 978－7－5520－4101－9

Ⅰ.①2… Ⅱ.①上… Ⅲ.①中央商业区—经济发展—研究报告—上海—2022 Ⅳ.①F727.51

中国国家版本馆CIP数据核字（2023）第050877号

2022 上海虹桥国际中央商务区发展报告

编　　者：上海虹桥国际中央商务区管理委员会
责任编辑：熊　艳
封面设计：黄婧昉
出版发行：上海社会科学院出版社
　　　　　上海顺昌路622号　邮编200025
　　　　　电话总机 021-63315947　销售热线 021-53063735
　　　　　http://www.sassp.cn　E-mail: sassp@sassp.cn
排　　版：南京展望文化发展有限公司
印　　刷：上海盛通时代印刷有限公司
开　　本：787毫米×1092毫米　1/16
印　　张：12.75
字　　数：260千
版　　次：2023年8月第1版　　2023年8月第1次印刷

ISBN 978-7-5520-4101-9 / F · 726　　　　　定价：108.00元